CITIES AND LANGUAGES: GOVERNANCE AND POLICY

An International Symposium

INVENIRE BOOKS

I NVENIRE is an Ottawa-based "idea factory" specializing in collaborative governance and stewardship. INVENIRE and its authors offer creative and practical responses to the challenges and opportunities faced by today's complex organizations.

INVENIRE BOOKS welcomes a range of contributions – from conceptual and theoretical reflections, ethnographic and case studies, and proceedings of conferences and symposia, to works of a very practical nature – that deal with problems or issues on the governance and stewardship front. INVENIRE BOOKS publishes works in French and English.

This is the eleventh volume published by INVENIRE BOOKS.

INVENIRE also publishes a quarterly electronic journal, found at www.optimumonline.ca.

Editorial Committee
Caroline Andrew
Robin Higham
Ruth Hubbard
Daniel Lane
Gilles Paquet (Chair)

The titles published by INVENIRE BOOKS are listed at the end of this book.

CITIES AND LANGUAGES: GOVERNANCE AND POLICY
An International Symposium

EDITED BY

RICHARD CLÉMENT & CAROLINE ANDREW

Proceedings of the international symposium,
"Language Planning in Capitals and Urban Environments,"
held March 25-26, 2010 at the University of Ottawa,
with sponsorship from the Official Languages and
Bilingualism Institute, Canadian Heritage, the Office of the
Commissioner of Official Languages and the City of Ottawa

INVENIRE BOOKS
Ottawa, Canada
2012

University of Ottawa Press
Les **Presses** de l'Université d'Ottawa

The University of Ottawa Press (UOP) is proud to be the oldest of the francophone university presses in Canada and the oldest bilingual university publisher in North America. Since 1936, UOP has been enriching intellectual and cultural discourse by producing peer-reviewed and award-winning books in the humanities and social sciences, in French and in English.

www.Press.uOttawa.ca

Library and Archives Canada Cataloguing in Publication

Title: Cities and languages : governance and policy : an international symposium / edited by Richard Clément & Caroline Andrew.
Names: International Symposium «Language Planning in Capitals and Urban Environments» (2010 : Ottawa, Ont.), author. | Clément, Richard, 1951- editor. | Andrew, Caroline, editor.
Description: Reprint. Originally published: Ottawa : Invenire Books, 2012. | Proceedings of the international symposium, "Language Planning in Capitals and Urban Environments," held March 25-26, 2010 at the University of Ottawa, with sponsorship from the Official Languages and Bilingualism Institute, Canadian Heritage, the Office of the Commissioner of Official Languages and the City of Ottawa. | Includes bibliographical references.
Identifiers: Canadiana (print) 20220389454 | Canadiana (ebook) 20220389497 | ISBN 9780776638287 (softcover) | ISBN 9780776638294 (PDF) | ISBN 9780776638300 (EPUB)
Subjects: LCSH: Language planning—Europe—Congresses. | LCSH: Language planning—Canada—Congresses. | LCSH: Language policy—Europe—Congresses. | LCSH: Language policy—Canada—Congresses. | LCSH: Capitals (Cities)—Europe—Congresses. | LCSH: Capitals (Cities)—Canada—Congresses. | LCGFT: Conference papers and proceedings.
Classification: LCC P40.5.L352 E85 2022 | DDC 306.44/94—dc23

Legal Deposit: Library and Archives Canada, Third Quarter 2022
© University of Ottawa Press 2022, all rights reserved.

This book was initially published by Invenire Books in 2012. The cover design, layout and design were produced by Sandy Lynch. Cover image by Zig8 (Dreamstime.com). The University of Ottawa Press reissued this book thanks to the support of Ontario Creates.

Invenire

Invenire Books, an Ottawa-based idea factory that operated from 2010 to 2019, specialized in collaborative governance and stewardship. Invenire and its authors provide creative practical and stimulating responses to the challenges and opportunities faced by today's organizations. The list is now carried by the University of Ottawa Press.

Profession: Public Servant
The Entrepreneurial Effect: Practical Ideas from Your Own Virtual Board of Advisors
La flotte blanche : histoire de la compagnie de navigation du Richelieu et d'Ontario
Tableau d'avancement II : essais exploratoires sur la gouvernance d'un certain Canada français
The Entrepreneurial Effect: Waterloo
The Unimagined Canadian Capital: Challenges for the Federal Capital Region
The State in Transition: Challenges for Canadian Federalism
Cities as Crucibles: Reflections on Canada's Urban Future
Gouvernance communautaire : innovations dans le Canada français hors Québec
Through the Detox Prism: Exploring Organizational Failures and Design Responses
Cities and Languages: Governance and Policy – An International Symposium
Villes et langues : gouvernance et politiques – symposium international
Moderato Cantabile: Toward Principled Governance for Canada's Immigration Policy
Stewardship: Collaborative Decentred Metagovernance and Inquiring Systems
Challenges in Public Health Governance: The Canadian Experience
Innovation in Canada: Why We Need More and What We Must Do to Get It
Challenges of Minority Governments in Canada
Gouvernance corporative : une entrée en matières

Tackling Wicked Policy Problems: Equality, Diversity and Sustainability
50 ans de bilinguisme officiel : défis, analyses et témoignages
Unusual Suspects: Essays on Social Learning
Probing the Bureaucratic Mind: About Canadian Federal Executives
Tableau d'avancement III : pour une diaspora canadienne-française antifragile
Autour de Chantal Mouffe : le politique en conflit
Town and Crown: An Illustrated History of Canada's Capital
The Tainted-Blood Tragedy in Canada: A Cascade of Governance Failures
Intelligent Governance: A Prototype for Social Coordination
Driving the Fake Out of Public Administration: Detoxing HR in the Canadian Federal Public Sector
Tableau d'avancement IV : un Canada français à ré-inventer
A Future for Economics: More Encompassing, More Institutional, More Practical
Pasquinade en F : essais à rebrousse-poil
Building Bridges: Case Studies in Collaborative Governance in Canada
Scheming Virtuously: The Road to Collaborative Governance
A Lantern on the Bow: A History of the Science Council of Canada and its Contributions to the Science and Innovation Policy Debate
Fifty Years of Official Bilingualism: Challenges, Analyses and Testimonies
Irregular Governance: A Plea for Bold Organizational Experimentation
Pasquinade in E: Slaughtering Some Sacred Cows

The University of Ottawa Press gratefully acknowledges the support extended to its publishing list by the Government of Canada, the Canada Council for the Arts, the Ontario Arts Council, the Social Sciences and Humanities Research Council and the Canadian Federation for the Humanities and Social Sciences through the Awards to Scholarly Publications Program, and by the University of Ottawa.

ONTARIO ARTS COUNCIL
CONSEIL DES ARTS DE L'ONTARIO
an Ontario government agency
un organisme du gouvernement de l'Ontario

Canada Council   Conseil des arts
for the Arts   du Canada

Canada

uOttawa

TABLE OF CONTENTS

LIST OF CONTRIBUTORS

Caroline Andrew, University of Ottawa (Canada)

Maria Björnberg-Enckell, City of Helsinki (Finland)

Emili Boix-Fuster, University of Barcelona (Spain)

Daniel Bourgeois, Beaubassin Research Institute (Moncton, Canada)

Aaron Burry, City of Ottawa (Canada)

Guy Chaisson, Université du Québec en Outaouais (Canada)

Richard Clément, University of Ottawa (Canada)

Gemma Cots, University of Barcelona (Spain)

Jordi Font, City of Barcelona (Spain)

Graham Fraser, Commissioner of Officials Languages of Canada

Philippe Hambye, Université catholique de Louvain (Brussels, Belgium)

Sylvie A. Lamoureux, University of Ottawa (Canada)

Pierre-Yves Moeschler, City of Biel/Bienne (Switzerland)

Antoni Rodon, City of Barcelona (Spain)

Georgina Rufo, University of Barcelona (Spain)

Christina Späti, University of Fribourg (Switzerland)

Colin H. Williams, Cardiff University (Wales)

PREFACE

Language Planning in Capitals and Urban Environments

Graham Fraser, Commissioner of Official Languages of Canada

Over 40 years ago, Canada took decisive action concerning the country's linguistic future. By adopting the *Official Languages Act*, the country chose to go against the trend toward homogeneity, and made equality of English and French a fundamental principle of Canadian society that the federal government had to advance, respect and promote. Enacted in the wake of the Royal Commission on Bilingualism and Biculturalism (the Laurendeau-Dunton Commission), which sought to shed light on the malaise felt by francophones in the country, the 1969 act marked the beginning of a new chapter in the history of the relationship that Canadian anglophones and francophones have with their government.

Four decades later, there is no longer any doubt that linguistic duality is a fundamental part of Canadian society. Over the years, it has shaped the way Canadians see themselves. It has also shaped the way Canada presents itself to the world: as a bilingual country that celebrates its linguistic duality by devoting as much of its energy to the French-speaking world as it does to the Commonwealth. Many individual representatives, from majority and minority communities and government organizations and institutions, have worked hard to make significant progress in advancing the equal status of both language communities.

Other individuals are now asking themselves how they can contribute to the Canadian linguistic duality. At the same time, some observers are trying to mobilize new players who are often deeply affected by Canadian linguistic duality but not very involved in promoting it. This led to the idea of holding an international symposium on cities and language planning.

In the same spirit as the Laurendeau-Dunton Commission, which focused on the international scene to better understand the Canadian language situation and put it into perspective, the "Language Planning in Capitals and Urban Environments" symposium sought to bring together administrators and researchers from Canadian and European cities to discuss language planning in urban environments. Initiating this dialogue was all the more important because current theoretical and practical knowledge on the subject is somewhat inconsistent and disjointed.

The exercise proved to be extremely productive. I found the breadth and depth of the presentations, discussions and ideas to be inspirational. Despite the sometimes very disparate circumstances and approaches, everyone came away with a better understanding of the issues. A number of topics were covered, from immigration to the role of the private sector, to the need to encourage dialogue between language communities. I would like to focus for a moment on one topic in particular: municipal bilingualism as a distinguishing asset.

As much through its architecture, its aromas and its climate as through its inhabitants, each city acquires an image and an identity. A city's image seems to matter more and more these days, whether it has evolved over time without any real planning or has been deliberately created. Thus, it was only a matter of time before municipal governments started to examine the image that their cities were projecting. If administrations are not proactive in creating an image for their city, then it is likely that citizens and visitors will do it for them.

During the symposium, some administrators and researchers invited cities to focus on their linguistic capital. Municipal bilingualism should be perceived as an asset that deserves to be promoted, rather than merely a question of regulation. Bilingualism is a symbol of openness and inclusion that cities can use to distinguish themselves from their neighbours.

By placing linguistic duality at the heart of its identity and image, a city encourages language communities to participate fully in its social, cultural and economic life, and inspires citizens and visitors alike to discover its many treasures.

Approaching municipal bilingualism as an asset to be promoted requires strong leadership and the ongoing cooperation of municipal authorities, the private sector and the community. Everyone must participate because everyone stands to gain. Promoting linguistic duality such that it becomes an integral part of a city's image and identity leads to major commercial, economic and cultural returns. It also fosters tourism and makes inhabitants feel proud to live in a city that reflects who they are. The benefits go beyond the merely symbolic.

Globalization often puts cities in competition with each other to attract potential investors, and many companies are now looking for personnel who are fluent in both official languages. In this context, bilingualism is an asset that can help a city distinguish itself.

Making linguistic duality an inherent part of a city's identity and image also instils good language instincts among its citizens, institutions and businesses, especially when it comes to considering both language communities in event planning, staffing or government project planning. Managers will set a good example by using the preferred language of the people they are addressing. This kind of behaviour fosters a sense of belonging and reinforces linguistic identity, while promoting harmony among citizens – essential ingredients to everyone's happiness.

Canada's cities are playing a new part in its political architecture and are increasingly being called upon to be bold and creative. Regardless of the issue – sustainable development, culture, immigration or even affordable housing – municipalities are finding new ways to meet new challenges. Symposium participants invited Canadian cities to view linguistic duality as a chance to showcase their assets.

I think this invitation deserves our full attention. A huge field of opportunity is opening up to Canadian municipalities, and most have yet to take advantage of it. Historically, cities have shied away from promoting linguistic duality. Maybe they preferred not to go down that controversial road, despite its enormous potential. This concern, albeit legitimate, should not stop municipalities from acting. On the contrary, this is a challenge that requires strong leadership.

Ottawa: A bilingual nation's capital

In 2010, the national capital region was ranked by *MoneySense* magazine as the best place to live out of 179 Canadian cities. It was also ranked first in 2007 and 2008 with populations over 10,000 people, and just missed top spot in 2009. In conducting the survey, the magazine looked at 24 factors ranging from average housing prices to air quality to crime rate.[1] Regardless of whether you agree with the methodology, the exercise makes you think about the factors that define quality of life. What makes people feel good in a city? In the country's capital?

[1] http://www.moneysense.ca/2010/04/30/best-places-to-live-2010/.

Canadians and newcomers all have hopes and expectations when it comes to their capital city, and they feel a certain pride in it as well. Ottawa is unique in Canada: it is a crossroads where our government, our identity and our international influence come together. In this sense, the nation's capital assumes an additional level of importance and responsibility.

As the commissioners of the Laurendeau-Dunton Commission said 40 years ago:

> ... a capital is a symbol of the country as a whole. It should express, in the best way possible, the values of the country as a whole, its way of life, its cultural richness and diversity, its social outlook, its aspirations for the future. This symbolism has both an internal and an external dimension. Citizens from across the country who visit their capital should find in it a fuller understanding of their country's traditions and a pride in personal identification with it. Similarly, visitors from other countries should be able just as readily to find tangible expression of the values of a country with which they may be unfamiliar.[2]

The Laurendeau-Dunton Commission also revealed how a large portion of the Canadian population felt about the nation's capital: many francophones did not feel at home there. Four decades later, we can appreciate how far we have come. Efforts made and accomplishments achieved must be acknowledged. There is still a lot of work to be done, however, so that both official languages can be seen and heard in the city's public spaces.

As a capital city that has been rated the best place to live in Canada and where more than a third of the population speaks both of our official languages, Ottawa has many great qualities, and bilingualism is definitely one of them.

Next steps

This symposium was the result of partnerships between various organizations and highlighted the need for forums, both in Canada and abroad, where administrators and experts in urban language planning can share knowledge and best practices. I hope it is the first of many. Publication of the symposium's proceedings marks the first important step in organizing and disseminating knowledge in this new field. The papers presented in the following pages will be a source of information and inspiration to those who work to promote bilingualism in their cities.

[2] Report of the Royal Commission on Bilingualism and Biculturalism. *Book V: The Federal Capital*, 1970, p. 3.

References

MoneySense staff. 2010. "Best Places to Live 2010". *MoneySense*, April 30, http://www.moneysense.ca/2010/04/30/best-places-to-live-2010/ [accessed November 14, 2011].

Report of the Royal Commission on Bilingualism and Biculturalism. 1970. *Book V: The Federal Capital*, Ottawa: Queen's Printer, p. 3.

INTRODUCTION

Language Policies and Bilingualism in Urban Environments: Situated Discussions

Sylvie A. Lamoureux and Richard Clément

This publication contains the proceedings of the international symposium "Language Planning in Capitals and Urban Environments: Practices and Challenges" that was held in Ottawa, Canada, March 25-26, 2010, and brought together university researchers and city administrators from six cities and capital regions in Canada and Europe: Barcelona, Biel/Bienne, Brussels, Helsinki, Moncton and the host city, Ottawa. The symposium was made possible through the cooperation of the University of Ottawa's Official Languages and Bilingualism Institute (OLBI) and Centre on Governance, the City of Ottawa's French Language Services Branch, and the Government of Canada's Department of Canadian Heritage and Office of the Commissioner of Official Languages.

The organizing committee shares, in part, the vision of Herberts and Turi (1999), who chaired and ran the Sixth International Conference on Law and Language in September 1998 in Vaasa, Finland. It was their view that it is essential to have university researchers and city administrators gather in one place to spark discussion, share successful practices that might be adapted and used by other polities, and identify research avenues and discussion topics to explore in international collaborative networks and local communities. Three common themes were discussed in a forum in which all invited participants and members of the public were free to take the floor and express their views. These themes were: administrative management and public services, symbolic representation and public image, and civic and institutional engagement.

The following chapters present two points of view: administrators describe their city's history and challenges; and researchers present critical thinking on their city's situation in light of the discussions on the symposium's three common themes.

The texts before you are not transcripts of the presentations, but instead summaries of the presenters' contributions. This material will be of interest to administrators, researchers and anyone interested in language policy and planning in multilingual urban environments, since it reveals the similarities and differences in the major issues faced by the six "bilingual" cities or capital regions. The texts are not intended to provide answers, but rather ideas and questions to generate discussion.

The concept of "city"

Calvet (2004: 17) states that "[in translation] a city is by definition a place of language variation and contact ... a place in which conflicts arise and communication problems find vehicular solutions." Calvet wrote the above as part of a discussion on the origin of sociolinguistics; however, the statement also shows us that the city is a place in which multilingualism can be found in everyday communication (Ibid.: 19). Multilingualism or the emergence of language vehicularity originated on trade routes and at ports, but it is in multilingual cities that the emergence of vehicularity and its effect on the status and corpus of languages is most noticeable (Ibid.: 19).

Gasquet-Cyrus (2004: 57) defines "city" as follows:

[In translation] ... *the physical materialization of human desires – money, work, social interaction, recreation, culture. ... The definition of "city" is economic, social and even political. Because speakers are socially diverse, languages play a social role; however, cities are not regulated by languages: languages are governed by urban social structuring.*

Social, political and economic structuring are therefore areas to explore, keeping in mind the high degree of human mobility characteristic of the start of the 21st century, which is transforming private and public spaces in cities. In diglossic environments, which languages should urban structuring promote? In officially unilingual or bilingual environments, how can multilingualism and speaker mobility be taken into account to meet the needs of residents? Should a city reflect the languages of its citizens and residents, or should the citizens and residents adapt to the city's way of structuring and managing language resources? To what extent should language resources be formally managed?

Issue, problem or question

The discussions at this symposium were not aimed at presenting bilingualism or linguistic diversity as a "problem". Grin (1990), Vaillancourt (1985), and Grin and Vaillancourt (1997) have long since pointed out the socio-economic benefits of multilingualism for individuals and for society. Our goal was to create a forum for dialogue on issues related to administrative realities and the offer of public services in a multilingual environment, on public image, on symbolic representation, and on commitment in polities in which the languages spoken have different statuses and individual bilingualism becomes more varied as a result of a multilingual society.

However, subtractive bilingualism or bilingualism as a means to achieve unilingualism (i.e., assimilation) has been identified as a challenge to be overcome in all the regions represented, especially with regard to education. Bilingual schools are perceived as places for interaction and the creation of social cohesion; however, studies of French-speakers in Canada (Churchill, Frenette and Quazi 1985; Landry 1995) show that unilingual schools are important to the vitality of the language minority. How can one reconcile the vision of the school as an ideal place for language contact on one hand and a protected place for language minorities on the other?

Language contact, interaction, diglossia

Our discussions on language planning inevitably led to the topic of the tension between bilingual individuals and multilingual societies that arises from the multiple linguistic realities of those living in places in which some languages are legally recognized and others are not, especially with regards to education. That tension has already been observed by Laponce (1996), Grin (1990), Nelde (2000) and, more recently, Mondada (2007), Moyer and Martin Rojo (2007) and others, who have documented the effect and social realities of a transnational shift. That shift is leading to a significant increase in multilingualism in urban areas. However, it is not yet moving toward the formal recognition of the status of other languages within the political region (whether the polity is officially bilingual or not, e.g., the City of Ottawa), nor to the recognition of rights for city residents. The discussions therefore addressed issues at two levels of planning: official language communities and multilingual societies.

As noted by Nelde (2000), it is not the languages that are in contact, but the speakers. A symmetric urban multilingualism does not exist, despite the ideal cosmopolis proposed by Gupta (2000). The official spaces of a city in which citizens gain access to services are not free of conflict, whether economic, political or other. Even if we consider bilingualism or multilingualism, a review of the literature on language interaction in urban environments by Dionne and Shulman (2007) highlights the diverse relationships between language agents, and shows how positive or reverse discrimination, decentralization, territorialization, enablement (Nelde 2000) and official multilingualism make it possible for residents who speak an officially recognized language to function as unilingual individuals in the multilingual municipal space.

The discussions at this symposium also inevitably led to the topic of the diglossic realities of urban areas in which even government policies and legislation cannot eliminate the realities of 'dominant' languages and 'dominated' languages, nor prevent the conflicts associated with the social mobility realities of minority groups. In Brussels, "personal matters" are managed by the two major language communities; however, in other communities, the majority manages the minority. Brussels is therefore home to few bilingual institutions; most institutions are completely unilingual, serving one of the two groups. Areas of true language contact in that environment are few, unlike in cities such as Barcelona, Moncton or Ottawa.

Aside from national and official languages, the transnational shift is adding complexity to the offer of services by increasing the number of languages spoken by those sharing the urban space and municipal resources. Even the principle of territoriality, as implemented in Switzerland, must deal with new linguistic realities, aside from the officially recognized language groups and the residents officially recognized as citizens entitled to participate in civic politics. Language contact in urban environments must be revisited in light of all interaction, and not only in diglossic terms.

Language ecology and networks

Fuentes-Calle (2007) proposes the viewpoint of multilingual networks to conceptualize the urban space, where the existence of areas in which people congregate based on language makes it possible for polities to target service delivery by language spoken. That refers, in a way, to Haugen's concept of language ecology (Haugen 1972), i.e., an exploration of the relationship between speakers and the diverse languages of a region, between the speakers of those languages and the social structures and services in which those languages are recognized and used (Blackledge 2008; Creese, Martin and Hornberger 2008). Networks would make it possible to identify locations for community health centres and schools for language minorities. However, what should be done if language communities are dispersed or critical mass has not been achieved? Should official minority language communities and language communities with critical mass be the only ones recognized? Should all languages be recognized and accommodated? The ecology viewpoint may make service delivery easier, but can it ensure the vitality and promotion of minority language communities and culture?

Accommodate or legislate?

We know that the most effective protection for language minorities are those entrenched in national or provincial (regional) legislation and case law. Nonetheless, the discussions at this symposium highlighted the importance of and the will to explore ways to better meet the needs of urban citizens of various language groups, whether official language minorities or not, through formal (such as bylaws and legislation) and informal means, with respect to place names, access to education and other issues.

The jurisdictions of the municipal governments represented at this symposium differed greatly from one country to another. What brought them together was their shared concern about the civic involvement of their citizens, the delivery of and access to a variety of services, and, especially, the social cohesion of all citizens sharing an urban space.

A number of issues were raised and identified as important discussion topics for the meetings to follow. Should the purpose of managing multilingualism in urban environments be to provide various language groups with equal access to services and civic involvement or equitable access? Should service delivery and civic involvement be limited to official language groups? What about promoting the vitality of language groups whether or not they are officially recognized and protected? What about the link between language and culture?

The discussions at this symposium also highlighted the significant tension between accommodating language groups and minorities in practice and granting official recognition (with all the services that that entails) through regulations or municipal bylaws. Those issues are primarily political and tied to the will to act. Hambye states that choosing a purely legal path assumes a political consensus rather than revealing a political compromise. However, finding a balance between accommodation and legislation should be discussed in a transnational context, in the context of the shift that is characteristic of the start of 21st century. The tension, between the bilingual individual and the multilingual society, where multilingualism is a reality in social and public life in the public and private sectors for individuals and society, is a common thread in the concerns and challenges of the cities taking part in this symposium.

The papers

Rather than arrange the papers by city, we thought it appropriate to show the development of the topics discussed above by arranging the papers according to their main focus. The first paper by Boix-Fuster, Cots and Rufo opens part 1 and sets the stage for our discussion of bilingual cities. It raises most of the topics explored by the other papers. Boix et al. present an analysis of Barcelona that touches on numerous aspects – historical, legal and demographic – while contrasting official languages with languages spoken. The second paper by Bourgeois focuses specifically on English-French bilingualism in Moncton. Bourgeois delves into an issue that is fundamental to all of the papers, namely, the issue of symbolic bilingualism, or façade. The third and fourth papers are about English-French bilingualism in the City of Ottawa. While both papers deal with similar topics, Burry takes the administrator's viewpoint and Andrew and Chiasson, the analysts'. Together, the two papers illustrate the counterpoint sought at this symposium between practice and critical thought. The fifth paper by Björnberg-Enckell deals mainly with bilingualism in Helsinki. It describes educational practices as the linchpin of formal municipal language planning.

Part 2 follows with four papers on bilingualism in multilingual environments in which the presence of languages, other than the official languages, significantly affects the structuring and implementation of language policies. Späti's paper on Biel/Bienne and Hambye's paper on Brussels describe the impact of policies based on the concept of territory, the obstacles and potential solutions. Both papers, the second more critically than the first, examine politics and economics in combination to provide us with an understanding of developments in the two cities. Font's paper on Barcelona deals with bilingualism in a multilingual environment, in which language borders are more spread out. It describes the administrative practices of a highly multi-ethnic city and presents a service delivery model and a number of examples. Lastly, Moeschler's paper on Biel/Bienne goes further with the concept of contact by contrasting the effects of territorial policies with the effects of repeated interaction between what are ultimately minority and majority groups. It also looks at the issue of migration patterns.

Finally, a conclusion by Colin Williams identifies issues emerging from our discussions that, we hope, will be catalysts for future exploration.

References

Blackledge, A.J. 2008. "Language Ecology and Language Ideology," in *Ecology of Language*, edited by A. Creese, P. Martin and N.H. Hornberger. *Encyclopedia of Language and Education*, vol 9. Heidelberg: Kluwer, pp. 2923-2936.

Bulot, T., ed. 2004. *Lieux de ville et identité*. vol. 1 of *Perspectives en sociolinguistique urbaine*. Paris: L'Harmattan.

Calvet, L.-J. 2004. "La sociolinguistique et la ville. Hasard ou nécessité?" in *Lieux de ville et identité. Perspectives en sociolinguistique urbaine*, edited by T. Bulot, vol. 1. Paris: L'Harmattan, pp. 14-29.

Churchill, S., N. Frenette and S. Quazi. 1985. *Éducation et besoins des franco-ontariens : Le diagnostique d'un système d'éducation*, vols. 1 and 2. Toronto: Conseil d'éducation franco-ontarien.

Dionne, E. and J. Shulman. 2007. "État des lieux : l'interaction des langues en milieu urbain." Internal report, Official Languages and Bilingualism Institute, University of Ottawa.

Fuentes-Calle, A. 2007. "Multilingual Cities: Rethinking Linguistic Diversity." http://www.wilsoncenter.org.

Gasquet-Cyrus, M. 2004. "Sociolinguistique urbaine ou urbanisation de la sociolinguistique? Regards critiques et historiques sur la sociolinguistique," in *Lieux de ville et identité. Perspectives en sociolinguistique urbaine*, edited by T. Bulot, vol. 1. Paris: L'Harmattan, pp. 31-69.

Grin, F. 1990. "The Economic Approach to Minority Languages," *Journal of Multilingual and Multicultural Development*, 11: 153-171.

Grin, F. and F. Vaillancourt. 1997. "The Economics of Multilingualism: Overview and Analytical Framework," *Annual Review of Applied Linguistics*, 17: 43-65.

Gupta, A.F. 2000. "Bilingualism in the Cosmopolis," *International Journal of the Sociology of Language*, 143: 107-119.

Haugen, E. 1972. *The Ecology of Language*. Stanford: Stanford University Press.

Herberts, K. and J.G. Turi, eds. 1999. *Multilingual Cities and Language Policies: Proceedings from the Sixth International Conference on Law and Language: 10-12 September 1998, Vaasa, Finland = Villes plurilingues et politiques linguistiques : Actes de la sixième Conférence internationale sur le droit et la langue: 10-12 septembre 1998, Vasa, Finlande*. Vaasa: Åbo Akademi University.

Landry, R. 1995. "Éducation en faveur des minorités : un modèle théorique," in *Conseil de l'Europe : Rapports de l'Atelier sur la recherche pédagogique en faveur des minorités*. Bautzen: Council of Europe.

Laponce, J. 1996. *Loi de Babel et autres régularités des rapports entre langue et politique*. Lévis: Presses de l'Université Laval.

Mondada, L. 2007. "Bilingualism and the Analysis of Talk at Work: Code-switching as a Resource for the Organization of Action and Interaction," in *Bilingualism: A Social Approach*, edited by M. Heller. New York: Palgrave Macmillan, pp. 297-318.

Moyer, M.G. and L. Martin Rojo. 2007. "Language Migration and Citizenship: New Challenges in the Regulation of Bilingualism," in *Bilingualism: A Social Approach*, edited by M. Heller. New York: Palgrave Macmillan, pp. 137-160.

Nelde, P.H. 2000. "Prerequisites for a New European Language Policy," *Journal of Multilingual and Multicultural Development*, 21 (5): 442-450.

Vaillancourt, F., ed. 1985. *Économie et langue*. Québec: Conseil de la langue française.

PART 1: BILINGUAL CITIES

Barcelona: A Bivalent Multilingual City

Emili Boix-Fuster, Gemma Cots and Georgina Rufo

Introduction

> *The city (Barcelona) was about to become a sort of Dublin, officially bilingual where everybody learns Gaelic at school but where they only use English, certainly, with an Irish accent, of course* (Pijoan 2007: 20).

This article describes some aspects of Catalan-Spanish bilingualism in Barcelona, a city where the historically unbalanced conflict between Catalan and Spanish evolves towards a growing linguistic and cultural bivalence and hybridity.

Catalan legislation has tried to offset the overwhelming political and social predominance of Castilian (also called Spanish). In the same way that the national Spanish Constitution treats Castilian, two Catalan laws on language policy (1983 and 1998) and, even more importantly, a new Statute of Autonomy (2006), state that knowledge of Catalan is both a duty and a right (Milian 2009, 2010, at press). Catalan legislation considers both languages to be official, but gives a slight edge to Catalan. It is said to be the *"llengua pròpia"* or native language, so it can be used as a "normal" or favoured – the default – language. It is evident, nevertheless, that normal is an ambiguous term. What is clear is that Spanish cannot be excluded from official uses, even though Catalan is used predominantly in local and Catalan domains. Recently, a judgment of the Spanish Constitutional Court on the Statute of Autonomy of Catalonia not only prohibited the use of the word "nation" referring to Catalonia, but also the preferential role of Catalan, thus ensuring the hegemony of Spanish (Tribunal Constitucional de Espana 2010)

Barcelona

Spain has experienced a limited decentralization process, which tends to be minimized due to recent centripetal forces. Castilian is still a privileged language. Catalan has still not been recognized as a national language on an equal footing with Castilian. Since the return of democracy in the late seventies, Catalan has become an official language again in Catalonia, together with Castilian, which is an official language throughout Spain. Catalan has entered the educational system, the local and regional public services, and some sectors of the mass media (McRoberts 2001). At the end of compulsory education, students have to master both official languages. Therefore, knowledge of Catalan (not necessarily its use) has increased significantly (Prats 2008).

Today Barcelona is the centre of an urban area of approximately four and a half million people, that is to say, 70 percent of the total population of Catalonia, the "autonomous community" of which it is the capital. Its current linguistic repertoire is the result of two factors. On the one hand, it has suffered severe and lasting political subordination to central Spain and, on the other hand, the bulk of its working class population comes from southern Spain, and is thus Castilian-speaking, sharing the language of the dominant Spanish state.

Barcelona is a place where, for example, if you carry out a small survey in the bar around the corner, each customer will give you a different answer to the question of what Catalonia is: a nation, a region, an autonomous community, a stateless territory, a piece of Spain and so on. The fate of Catalan is sometimes a topic in everyday discourse and in literature as per the initial citation, both of which forecast its decay much like Irish in Dublin. Barcelona citizens face up to so many challenges in everyday life (health, ageing, unemployment, housing ...) that only rarely is there public discussion of language choices. There is recurrent double talk, though. Whereas the defenders of bilingualism ("Partido Popular," the Spanish nationalist conservative party) only pay lip service to it, and really defend the supremacy of Castilian, Catalan militants are expected to be bilingual; they are reluctant to promote generalized bilingualism because they are afraid that this will mean Castilian-speakers would remain unilingual.

From the outset it must be pointed out that there is no clear dominant or minority language in Barcelona. On the one hand, for political, legal and economic reasons, Castilian is the first language. The Spanish Constitution (1978, article 3), for instance, establishes that all Spanish citizens have both the right and the duty to know Castilian. The Spanish market works in Castilian: all products can be labelled only in Castilian because all Spaniards, without exception, know this language. On the other hand, Catalan was the oldest and original language in Catalonia, before linguistic repression and migration waves took place.

Symbolic representations and public image

Barcelona is no doubt the centre of Catalonia, not only because it is the capital of the autonomous community. Indeed, the communication networks (transportation, telephone lines, daily mobility and commuting) of all of Catalonia hinge on the city: the main universities and businesses are located there; FC Barcelona, the victorious soccer team, plays in the city and rallies the spirits of the Catalans, from whatever village and city. The contemporary vitality of Catalan as a vernacular language, despite centuries of institutional inferiority, is unique among the lesser used languages of Western Europe. This is especially noteworthy in light of the repression of the Franco years (1939-1975), where there were concerted attempts to eradicate the language. The Catalan case is a counter-example to the generalization that lesser-used languages erode in industrialized, urban societies.

The city of Barcelona has two sociolinguistic images. On the one hand, one could say that Catalan has survived because its capital has maintained the language. Robert Hughes (1993), the author of a recognized literary guide to the city, chose as a title for a chapter in his book "Blind with love for a language". Maybe the city's inhabitants are not concerned with these issues on a daily basis, but many of them have shown themselves to be loyal to their language. For example, the city has been the centre of language reform movements (Costa 2009). On the other hand, there is a sort of *méfiance*, a mistrust, between Barcelona and its Catalan hinterland, because of, above all, its demographic unbalance and its different linguistic and political orientations. From 1980 to 2003, Catalonia was ruled by a moderate centre-right pro-autonomy coalition (CiU), whereas Barcelona has been ruled ever since by a social democratic party (PSC(PSC-PSOE)). The first coalition emphasized the struggle to maintain and enhance Catalan identity, whereas the socialists emphasized a multicultural, multi-ethnic vision of the city. For the other Catalans, Barcelona appears as relatively more Castilianized than Catalonia as a whole, even though the city's figures show a higher use and knowledge of the language than in its metropolitan area.

Generally speaking, the social democrats have not shown much interest in emphasizing the main ethnolinguistic boundaries within the city between those having Catalan as their first and preferred language, and those having Castilian as their first and preferred language (Woolard 2009). The Institute of Metropolitan Studies (under social democratic control as well) alone has been interested in linguistic identity, but offers little linguistic information on the 38 Barcelona neighbourhoods (Subirats

2002). Therefore, the available data on Barcelona are limited. They deal mainly with the knowledge of Catalan in the 10 districts of the city (each district contains a given number of neighbourhoods), and much less on the first language or language of national identity. Only in 2003 and 2005 (Boix 2005) was a map drawn, showing the percentages of people speaking and understanding Catalan in the neighbourhoods of the city. Moreover, in its almost eighty issues, the journal *Barcelona Metrópolis*, the mouthpiece of the municipality in cultural affairs, has never addressed in any depth the linguistic diversity of the city.

We do not possess, therefore, an overall picture of the linguistic landscape of the city similar to Gorter (2006), only the seminal work of Bertran (2005). Some hypotheses have been put forward, but they need to be verified through further research. *First*, that Catalan is more widely used in institutionalized domains than in private, interpersonal domains. Institutional communications are those which someone delivers or writes as member of an institution (a public servant, for example) (Bastardas 1996), whereas private communications are those uttered by someone in his or her private life. The priority given to Catalan in the local and autonomous administration and the demographic dominance of the Castilian speaking population would explain this imbalance. *Second*, and in a similar fashion, Catalan would be more common in *in vitro* uses than in *in vivo* uses. Castilian has become a deeply colloquialized code and many service workers are non-Catalan speaking immigrants. Likewise, Palou and Fons (2009) state that the school pays greater attention to formal and written varieties of Catalan than to informal and oral uses. *Third*, that the lack of everyday language conflict is due to the fact that most people are at least passively bilingual, so they can understand written and oral messages in both languages (Marí 1996). Only unilingual Castilian-speakers (there are no uniligual Catalan-speakers) force others to use their language. To sum up, asymmetrical bilingualism (more favourable to Spanish) still characterizes the city, even after decades of democracy and local language policy to encourage the use of Catalan.

Demolinguistic balance in urban environments

The demographic weight and the social distribution of each ethnolinguistic group in the city reveals an interesting story. The social distribution of Catalan and Castilian in Barcelona is sandwich-like. Castilian is the language of a very thin, upper social class (McDonough 1986) and the dominant language among the working-class population, whereas Catalan predominates in the middle-class sectors. In 1996, for instance, Catalan was the language spoken to the mother by 39.9 percent of the citizens throughout the city (Subirats 1998). In five districts, this percentage of Catalan as mother tongue was higher than the average: namely in Gràcia (61.6 percent), Sarrià–Sant Gervasi (49.5 percent), Eixample (50.9 percent), Les Corts (43.9 percent) and Sants–Montjuïc (49.8 percent), whereas in other districts, the percentages were lower than the average: Ciutat Vella (34.7 percent), Nou Barris (17.9 percent), Sant Martí (37.3 percent), Sant Andreu (32.0 percent), and Horta–Guinardó (28.3 percent). This geographic and sociolinguistic distribution reflects the social stratification: the wealthiest districts are more Catalan-speaking and the poorest ones (those with more people of immigrant origin) are more Castilian-speaking, even though in the richest districts there is a slight recovery of Castilian (Subirats 2002; Boix 2003). Recent research on the linguistic landscape of the city shows a growing hybridity in signage in the city (Long and Comajoan 2010, personal communication). The two linguistic groups are still slightly socially segregated, even though political parties attempt continually to minimize this social cleavage. Marginalized groups still tend to be associated with Castilian (Woolard 2009). Most political parties are not organized along ethnolinguistic lines, even though Partido Popular and Ciudadanos play the role of defender of Castilian speakers.

While as we said earlier there are no recent data on first language and preferred identification language of the population in Barcelona, the geographic (and social) distribution of linguistic competence of the population (Ajuntament de Barcelona 2001) gives us some clues to the linguistic fabric of the city. The districts that show a higher percentage of understanding and speaking Catalan are those which tend to vote Convergència i Unió, the pro-Catalan centre-right coalition. Those districts with a lesser knowledge of Catalan, conversely, are those with a higher percentage of people not born in Catalonia or coming from immigrant families, and who tend to vote for the socialist party. Ciutat Vella, the old city, shows the lowest figures as far as knowledge of Catalan is concerned, because the majority of new immigrants are concentrated there. In this district, only 88.1 percent claim to understand Catalan, whereas, in the city as a whole, 95.1 percent claim to understand it. While the levels of understanding are very similar throughout all the districts, the percentages relating to the ability to speak Catalan are very different: only 59.8 percent in Ciutat Vella but 84.6 percent in Sarrià–Sant Gervasi. Finally, the figures concerning the ability to write are very low. A mere

47.1 percent of the whole population can write in Catalan. Here one can see traces of the repression of Catalan: most people were not allowed to learn Catalan at school.

The data on the differences in knowledge of Catalan according to age change dramatically. The percentages for knowledge of Catalan in all areas (understanding, speaking, reading and writing) are higher among the younger generations thanks to the addition of Catalan in the educational system. Whereas 89.2 percent of the respondents between 15 and 24 years can speak Catalan, only 62.6 percent of the oldest age group (65 and over) can do so. The differences are even more evident when we look to the data on writing: whereas 82.8 percent of the respondents between 15 and 24 years can write in Catalan, only 25.4 percent of those 65 years and over can do so.

In summary, in recent years Barcelona has undergone a process of "normalization," that is, knowledge of Catalan has clearly increased. But the prestige of Catalan has not been sufficient to recruit new Catalan-speaking members from the Castilian-speaking immigrant population or from the most recent immigrants on a large scale. Many of them still do not consider Catalan their own language (Subirats 2002). The Catalan language now faces new challenges in the Barcelona area. Subirats (2002) poses some questions about the recent new population: "The arrival of new [immigrants], a part of whom have Castilian as their language, raises doubts as to whether the Catalan language will have a sufficient demographic base to maintain itself as the language of an important part of the population if immigration strengthens the Castilian-speaking group tendency" (Ibid.: 187, in translation). Market and state forces within the globalization process endanger the prospects of the weakest language in the city, Catalan. Language policy measures seem to be insufficient.

The public services and the linguistic landscape

All these demo-linguistic changes have taken place in a particular legal framework which goes some way towards explaining the current linguistic landscape of Barcelona. In the institutionalized domains, which do not show a diglossic pattern, the main intervening variable is the area of government involved. For example, the services of the central government in Catalonia use Castilian preferably, because Catalan is not official in the central bodies of the Spanish government. These services include immigration offices and the branches of the central administration: social security, the tax offices, the post office, the military, and so on. The judicial system uses Castilian almost exclusively because judges are not required to learn Catalan. Conversely, institutions that depend on the autonomous or local Catalan governments, though bilingual, give a slight edge to Catalan.

As a result, the official street signs in Barcelona are mainly, but not exclusively, in Catalan. The taped messages in the subway cars are sometimes given in Catalan, sometimes in other languages, including Castilian, whereas the written announcements are trilingual (Catalan, Spanish and English). The main speeches by the city's mayor are mostly in Catalan. Local Barcelona TV is mainly in Catalan, but the big Spanish private channels broadcast only in Castilian. Parliamentary and municipal council sessions are normally held in Catalan. Political campaign advertisements, health information booklets or the notification of fines by the municipality, however, are either bilingual, sometimes only in Castilian, sometimes only in Catalan, in an erratic sort of way.

In private domains, Castilian is the dominant language, but not the only one. Although there are few studies available, in the workplace and in big companies and factories, Castilian is the first language. Church services (mainly Catholic) are in either language, with an important presence of Catalan. On the other hand, most commercial and economic information, for instance labelling of food, clothing and pharmaceutical products, is usually given only in Castilian. Most of the press is in Castilian: for example, the free press publishes a little under 15 percent of its articles in Catalan. However, announcements to the public at the Barcelona soccer club stadium are broadcast only in Catalan. The posters and signage in the markets are either in Castilian or Catalan, and are rarely bilingual in a parallel systematic way. An exception to this pattern is the leading Barcelona newspaper, El Periódico, which decided to launch a parallel edition in Catalan, identical to the original version in Castilian.

To date, most of these language use phenomena are *in vitro*; that is, they are the product of planned decisions, as opposed to *in vivo* phenomena, of a more spontaneous nature. Of course, the linguistic landscape is much more complicated. In a restaurant, for instance, the menus might be written in Catalan, but the Catalan customers tend to address waiters in Castilian, because many of them are recent immigrants, and because Catalan speakers have acquired this habit of using Castilian in public. In sports clubs, car driving schools or in the cinema, frequently the external written information (box offices, timetable information ...) is only in Catalan, whereas the spoken language of trainers, driving instructors and cinema employees is almost always Castilian. Funeral and death notices are either in Catalan or Castilian. Most informal everyday conversations are in Spanish, depending on the neighbourhood and the addressee.

We could say that there is a pervasive fluid bilingualism in Barcelona, with no strict rules or regulations, and, we dare to say, that there is some sort of linguistic confusion. This sort of bilingualism works because a clear majority of the population is at least passively bilingual.

In Barcelona as a whole, *in vivo* messages and individualized communications are mainly in Castilian, since Castilian has greater demo-linguistic weight, and also because inter-ethnic language norms encourage its use. The usual linguistic etiquette requires that Catalan speakers accommodate Castilian: they usually converge towards Spanish in bilingual encounters, though they will continue to speak in Catalan to a Catalan who is addressing Castilian-speaking participants. In speech addressed to non-identified interlocutors, for example, asking for directions or asking the time, both languages are commonly used in these interactions; it is assumed that the addressee will understand either language. In Barcelona, there is a clear struggle between each language's claim for a role as the anodyne language – as everybody's language – the public language, or *lingua franca* (Woolard 2008). So far, as a recent exposition (Aballí et al. 2010) proposes, the result is a "draw".

Conclusion

We have presented a very brief description of the linguistic repertoire of Barcelona. It is not easy to describe, much less to debate, the sociolinguistic situation in this urban area. Most inhabitants of the city consider the personal and collective benefits of preserving their historical language, Catalan, to be important in enhancing their self-esteem and positive self-image. The sociolinguistic landscape of Barcelona may appear complex, because there is not a unique, dominant language for all social functions, and because linguistic regulations are frequently flouted. Recently a new phenomenon has emerged: the arrival of new migrants, especially from Latin America and Morocco. Their integration is hindered by the precarious legal and economic situation in which many find themselves when they arrive. In addition to many social problems, it triggers a new sociolinguistic dilemma. Which local group will they join, the Catalan one or the Castilian one? Catalans, who speak a vulnerable language, feel that they may become a minority in their own territory if they don't succeed in spreading their language amongst newcomers. Immigrants could accelerate, not cause, the demise of Catalan.

References

Aballí, I. et al. 2010. *Barcelona, València, Palma. Una història de confluències i divergències* [Barcelona, Valencia, Palma: A history of convergences and divergences]. Barcelona: CCCB, Diputació de Barcelona and Generalitat de Catalunya.

Ajuntament de Barcelona, Departament d'Estadística. 2001. *Cens de Població i Habitatges 2001* [Population and Housing Census 2001]. Barcelona: Instituto Nacional de Estadística. Institut d'Estadística de Catalunya.

Bastardas, A. 1996. *Ecologia de les llengües. Medi. Contactes i dinàmica sociolingüística* [Ecology of languages. Medium. Contacts and sociolinguistic dynamics]. Barcelona: Proa.

Bertran, C. 2005. *Les veus de Barcelona: una aproximació a la realitat multilingüe de la ciutat* [The voices of Barcelona: an approximation to the multilingual reality of the city]. Paper presented at the *International Congress on Bilingualism*, Barcelona, March.

Boix, E. 2003. "Barcelone 2000: un état de la question sociolinguistique," in E. Boix and A. Milian (eds.), *Aménagement linguistique dans les pays de langue catalane*. Paris: L'Harmattan, pp. 13-243.

_____. 2005. "Català," in R. Alberch and J. Giralt (eds.), *Enciclopèdia de Barcelona*. Barcelona: Enciclopèdia Catalana-Ajuntament de Barcelona, pp. 282-286.

Costa, J. (ed.). 2009. *The Architect of Modern Catalan. Pompeu Fabra (1968-1948). Selected writings*. Amsterdam: John Benjamins.

Gorter, D. 2006. *Linguistic Landscape. A New Approach to Multilingualism*. Clevedon: Multilingual Matters.

Hughes, R. 1993. *Barcelona*. London: The Harvill Press.

Long, E. and L. Comajoan. 2010. "Linguistic landscape of three streets in Barcelona: Patterns of language visibility in public space," personal communication.

Marí, I. 1996. "La capital internacional de la llengua catalana" [The international capital of the Catalan language], in I. Marí (ed.), *Plurilingüisme europeu i llengua catalana*. València: Universitat de València, pp. 93-110.

McDonough, G.W. 1986. *Good Families in Barcelona. A Social History of Power in the Industrial Era.* Princeton: Princeton University Press.

McRoberts, K. 2001. *Catalonia. Nation Building Without a State.* Oxford: Oxford University Press.

Milian, A. (ed.). 2009. *El plurilingüisme a la Constitució espanyola* [Multilingualism in the Spanish constitution]. Barcelona: Institut d'Estudis Autonòmics.

_____. 2010. *Drets lingüístics per a tothom* [Linguistic rights for everyone]. Palma de Mallorca: Lleonard Muntaner.

_____. at press. "El régimen de las lenguas oficiales," comentario de la Sentencia del Tribunal Constitucional 31/2010 de 28 de junio [The regulation of the official languages, comment on the sentence by the Constitutional Court 31/2010]. *Revista Catalana de Dret Públic,* June 28.

Palou, J. and M. Fons. 2009. "Actituds dels docents davant de les noves situacions escolars multiculturals i multilingües: qüestions recurrents" [Teachers' attitudes towards the new multicultural and multilingual situations at school: recurrent issues], *Zeitschrift für Katalanistik,* 22: 151-169.

Pijoan, J. 2007. *Sayonara Barcelona.* [Good-Bye Barcelona]. Barcelona: Proa.

Prats, J. (ed.). 2008. *Estudi demogràfic i lingüístic de l'alumnat de 4t d'ESO de Catalunya. Avaluació de l'educació secundària obligatòria 2006.* [Demographic and linguistic research on the 4th grade students of Catalonia. Evaluation of the compulsory secondary education 2006]. Barcelona: Departament d'Educació, Generalitat de Catalunya.

Subirats, M. 1998. "Trets culturals: educació, llengua i hàbits de lleure" [Cultural characteristics: education, language and leisure habits], in O. Nel·lo *et al.* (eds.), *La transformació de la societat metropolitana. Una lectura de l'enquesta sobre condicions de vida i hàbits de la regió metropolitana de Barcelona (1985-1995).* Bellaterra: Institut d'Estudis Metropolitans, pp. 69-91.

_____. 2002. "Els trets lingüístics" [Linguistic characteristics], in S. Giner (ed.), *Enquesta de la Regió Metropolitana de Barcelona 2002.* Bellaterra: Institut d'Estudis Metropolitans, pp. 179-187.

Tribunal Constitucional de Espana. 2010. *Sentencia 31/2010 relativa al recurso de inconstitucionalidad contra la Ley Orgánica 6/2006, de 19 de julio, de reforma del Estatuto de Autonomía de Cataluña* [Sentence referring to the appeal against the law 6/2006, July 19, reforming the Statute of Autonomy of Catalonia]. June 28, 2010. Madrid: Suplemento del BOE del número 172, July 16, 2010.

Woolard, K.A. 2008. "Language and identity choice in Catalonia: The interplay of contrasting ideologies of linguistic authority," in K. Süselbeck, U. Mühlschlegel and P. Masson (eds.), *Lengua, Nación e Identidad. La regulación del plurilingüismo en España y América Latina.* Frankfurt a. Main: Vervuert, 303-323.

_____. 2009. "Linguistic Consciousness among Adolescents in Catalonia: A Case Study from the Barcelona Urban Area in Longitudinal Perspective," *Zeitschrift für Katalanistik,* 22: 125-149.

Moncton: Symbol of Bilingualism and Symbolic Bilingualism

Daniel Bourgeois

Introduction

In 2002, the City of Moncton became the first officially bilingual city in Canada. The symbolic declaration was unanimously approved by a city council that, 34 years earlier, had humiliated francophones. Moncton thus turned the page on a sad period in its history and became a Canada-wide symbol of municipal bilingualism. The symbolism, however, hides a secondary objective and limits progress in practice. A symbol can be a double-edged sword.

Background

In reality, Moncton has been a bilingual city since its incorporation in 1855. One hundred years after the Great Upheaval (Griffiths 2006), Acadians returned and settled alongside Anglo-Saxon families (Pincombe and Larracey 1990). Since that time, the city has been composed of two linguistic communities, with anglophones representing two thirds of the population, francophones, one third, and speakers of other languages, less than four percent.

However, despite that demo-linguistic history, Moncton had the appearance of a unilingual anglophone city until recently. Francophones were viewed (and many viewed themselves) as second-class citizens. They almost always had to express themselves in English in public, at work and when communicating with federal, provincial and municipal institutions. They had to send their children to bilingual schools bent on assimilation. They also had to create their own institutions: hospital, credit unions, insurance company, college and newspaper (Brun 1999). Their sizable critical mass ensured their survival, but did not guarantee tolerance or respect from the anglophone majority. The most popular public battleground was in the Canadian National rail shops, where members of the Orange Lodge and *Patente acadienne* fought for jobs.

The situation came to a head in February 1968, when a few students from Université de Moncton, an Acadian university founded in 1963, requested that city hall provide services and communications in French. The response from Mayor Jones and the majority of the anti-French city council came back loud and clear: francophones had to address the city council in English. In a subsequent demonstration, a pig's head was left in front of the mayor's office (LeBlanc 1996). The mayor went on to oppose official bilingualism in the Parliament of Canada as a member of Parliament from 1974 to 1979 and before the Supreme Court of Canada (*Jones v. New Brunswick* 1975). The Supreme Court case dealt with the legality of Canada's *Official Languages Act*; Jones' goal was to abolish official bilingualism in Canada and New Brunswick, because he considered the policy an affront to the anglophone majority and British parliamentary traditions. Jones became the symbol of the anti-bilingualism movement, and the fact that he held the position of mayor did not augur well for Acadians in Moncton. However, it was Jones' vehement opposition to bilingualism that motivated the city's Acadian advocates to continue to fight for linguistic equality. Their progress would not have been as rapid had it not been for Jones.

Thirty-four years later, after much significant but low-profile progress which included pro-French efforts initiated in 1971 by Mayor Jones and the city council as well as the policy on (bilingual) communications adopted in 1991, Moncton was proclaimed an officially bilingual city in an August 2002 declaration, unanimously approved by the city council, which was composed mainly of anglophones.[3] However, the declaration went no further. It required the city to "make all public notifications and information available in both official languages ... provide that the proceedings of City Council [be] conducted in both official languages while making simultaneous translation services available ... [and] provide municipal services to the public in both official languages;" however, those requirements were already set out in New Brunswick's *Official Languages Act*, which had been amended by the Legislative Assembly in June 2002, after the courts ruled against the City of Moncton in *Charlebois v. Moncton (City)* (2001). It appeared that the declaration was *only* symbolic.

Nevertheless, the declaration lanced the boil and freed the Acadian advocates. The declaration was approved by Moncton's Acadian leaders, as well as by businesses, the media, and the federal and provincial governments (Bourgeois 2010). As a result, since 2002, the city, business community and volunteer organizations have been improving their French-language services

[3] City of Moncton, *Declaration of Official Bilingualism*, August 6, 2002.

and communications, and have agreed to make French an important value. Though it may be only a superficial symbol, the declaration has played an important social role.

Symbol and symbolism

The work of Murray Edelman (1971) has shown that some policies are symbolic but play an important role. Nevertheless, a policy stating that a municipality is "bilingual" after the municipality has struggled with major language disputes cannot be downplayed. A policy can be criticized for being merely symbolic, but the 2002 declaration publicly bound the francophone and anglophone communities together in a common destiny. A wedding band is much more than a metal ring; it is the symbol of a union. After 150 years of disrespect, Acadians could finally express themselves in French in Moncton. In reality, they had been doing so increasingly since 1968, but the declaration made that reality official and, above all, showed that city hall was no longer a bastion of the anglophone establishment and that the city council would henceforth foster equal status for both official language communities.

In addition to its intrinsic symbolic value, the 2002 declaration enabled Moncton to present itself as a symbol of municipal bilingualism in Canada. A number of Canadian municipalities had declared themselves bilingual before 2002, but they were small and the linguistic minority (francophones living outside Quebec) formed a strong majority of their population. Moncton was the first city with a strong anglophone majority to declare itself bilingual. The declaration made national headlines and was praised *a mari usque ad mare*.[4] The city took the opportunity to encourage people and businesses to move to Moncton. The value of the municipal bilingualism symbol therefore extended beyond Moncton's city limits.

The Moncton declaration focuses on three levels of symbolism, each relating to a different area. Locally, it makes it possible to resolve language disputes in the city. Regionally, it removes a barrier to amalgamation. Amalgamation might result in services that are more efficient (one administration versus three), but would assimilate francophones in the urban centre. Currently, in Dieppe, an adjacent city, the francophone majority can manage the city's human, financial and physical resources in a way that supports its language, culture and community. An amalgamation would bring together the 14,000 Dieppe francophones, 21,000 Moncton francophones and 2,000 Riverview francophones, but they would represent

---

[4] Canada's motto: "from sea to sea."

only one third of the population. Furthermore, Dieppe council leaders are putting pressure on their Moncton counterparts regarding language issues. Nationally, the 2002 declaration raised the social and political profile of Moncton, enabling the city to promote its comparative advantages.

However, the declaration did not lead to the resolution of all language disputes in Moncton. In 2009, the city council was forced to amend the policy on (bilingual) communications for the third time.[5] First, the city council delegated to senior management the authority to designate bilingual positions. Previously, the city council had to approve the designation of each bilingual position in an open meeting, which gave some councillors the opportunity to make disparaging remarks about francophones and bilingualism. Next, the city council set out a clear assignment of responsibilities and accountability for bilingual communications and services. It also put the policy in a broader social context by making equal status for both linguistic communities the ultimate goal of the policy. As well, the city council added a clause requiring it to review the policy (read: increase the requirements) every five years. Lastly, it changed the policy's name to *Policy on Official Languages*, to clarify the kind of "communications" that it covered.

The symbolic declaration is in fact a double-edged sword. It makes it possible to turn the page on past events, especially the 1968 demonstrations, and free advocates of both linguistic communities, and promote bilingualism in Moncton as a benefit socially (quality of life) and economically (job creation). However, it hides a secondary objective, namely, the amalgamation of the three municipalities, which could weaken the Acadian community in the urban area, and it enables the city council to limit the declaration's symbolic value to the delivery of services and communications to the public.

The 2002 declaration was adopted not only for its intrinsic and extrinsic benefits, but also, in an underhanded way, to make it easier to amalgamate the City of Moncton with Dieppe that is 80 percent francophone. In 1992, the provincial government threatened to amalgamate Moncton, Dieppe and Riverview, but ultimately backed down in 1994, because Moncton was not sufficiently bilingual (Bourgeois 1995). Dieppe municipal councillors then launched a number of autonomy initiatives to keep Dieppe distinct from Moncton and avoid any potential threat of amalgamation (D. Bourgeois and Y. Bourgeois 2005). The 2002 symbolic declaration removed the largest barrier to amalgamation (Bourgeois 2005). In response, the Dieppe

[5] City of Moncton, *Policy on Official Languages*, August 2009.

municipal council stepped up its administrative nationalism (Bourgeois 2007) and passed a resolution in 2003 that declared Dieppe a francophone city (Y. Bourgeois and D. Bourgeois 2007). Therefore, while the Moncton declaration has made amalgamation possible again, the Dieppe declaration, which is just as symbolic, has presented an insurmountable obstacle to Moncton's amalgamation plans.

In addition, the 2002 declaration hampers progress toward linguistic equality. It recognizes the equal status of both languages, but limits progress to the "[provision of] municipal services to the public in both official languages". It therefore does away with other potential contributions by the city to equal status for its two languages, two cultures and two communities.

For example, the declaration does not deal with municipal place names. More than 90 percent of street names and public place names are English, which is at odds with the sociolinguistic reality. Furthermore, in recent years, the city has been removing the words "rue," "avenue" and "boulevard" before the name of certain main arteries, leaving only the English name, such as "Mapleton," "Vaughan Harvey" and "Killam." Place names are therefore becoming increasingly anglicized.

The declaration does not deal with commercial signs either. The linguistic landscape contributes to linguistic and cultural identity in minority communities (Landry, Deveau and Allard 2006; Boudreau and Dubois 2005). A number of other municipalities in the province are discussing the issue, and Dieppe recently passed a bylaw that requires new businesses to post information in French; however, the Moncton City Council is hesitating to become involved with the private sector.

The 2002 declaration does not encourage the City of Moncton to foster bilingualism in volunteer organizations that provide important services in the city, in particular, amateur sport organizations for youth. The city has not seen fit to offer assistance, especially in translating forms and websites into French. If those volunteer organizations were to disappear, however, the city would be required to provide those services in both official languages.

Lastly, the city is doing little to enable its francophone employees to work in French. The city council amended its policy on communications to give both languages equal status within its administration, but francophone employees are still communicating in English at meetings with unilingual anglophone colleagues. In fact, a number of francophone employees are communicating in English with each other.

However, progress is on the horizon. In 2008, the majority of the city council was francophone for the very first time. It is therefore likely that the city council's interpretation of the 2002 declaration will be broad rather than narrow, extending the declaration's scope beyond the delivery of services and communications. If that is the case, its practical scope will extend beyond the realm of a symbolic declaration. The 2009 version of the language policy provides the best example. Its objective is progress toward equal status for both languages, both cultures and both communities. As mentioned, the city council also added an incentive regarding the language of work. As well, the Dieppe commercial sign bylaw is pushing the Moncton City Council to work with business associations in the city to encourage businesses to post information in both languages. The Dieppe effort shows the significant role that can be played by a municipality with a francophone majority that accepts the challenge of fostering the linguistic and cultural development of its residents; it also shows the linguistic risk of amalgamation. If Dieppe were amalgamated with Moncton and Riverview, it is unlikely that the bylaw would have been passed. In addition, a number of francophone Moncton city councillors are working to increase the presence of French in place names. Finally, the new city manager, the first francophone to hold that position, has made a commitment to increase the use of French in municipal government operations. For now, the declaration remains symbolic and limited to municipal services and communications, but it appears that that narrow interpretation will be gradually discarded.

Conclusion

Since the 1968 demonstrations, the City of Moncton has made great linguistic progress, the most significant achievement of which is the symbolic 2002 declaration. However, that declaration, which makes Moncton a Canada-wide symbol of bilingualism, remains largely symbolic because its scope is limited in practice. The communications policy adopted in 1991, and amended in 2009, broadens the scope somewhat, and the city council is planning to act on commercial signs, municipal place names, volunteer organization support and language of work. Otherwise, the 2002 declaration will make Moncton a bilingual city officially but not in practice, and Moncton will be known for its symbolic municipal bilingualism rather than as a Canadian municipal symbol of bilingualism.

References

Boudreau, A. and L. Dubois. 2005. "L'affichage à Moncton : masque ou miroir?" *Revue de l'Université de Moncton*, 36: 185-217.

Bourgeois, D. 1995. "La décentralisation administrative de 1992 au Nouveau-Brunswick et le contrôle du territoire." *Égalité*, 38: 59-97.

_____. 2005. "Municipal Reforms in New Brunswick: To Decentralize or Not to Decentralize?" in *Municipal Reforms in Canada: Municipal Governance for the 21st Century*, ed. E. Lesage and J. Garcea. Don Mills: Oxford University Press, pp. 242-268.

_____. 2007. "Administrative nationalism," *Administration and Society*, 39: 631-655.

_____. 2010. "Moncton," in *Elements of Governance in Canada*, ed. B. Young and A. Sancton. Kingston and Montreal: McGill-Queen's University Press.

Bourgeois, D. and Y. Bourgeois. 2005. "Territory, Institutions and National Identity: The Case of Acadians in Greater Moncton, Canada," *Urban Studies*, 42: 1123-1138.

Bourgeois, Y. and D. Bourgeois. 2007. "La relation entre territoire et identité : Construction de l'identité acadienne et urbaine dans la région du Grand Moncton," in *Balises et références – Acadies, francophonies*, ed. M. Pâquet and S. Savard. Québec: Presses de l'Université Laval, pp. 105-126.

Brun, R. 1999. *Les Acadiens à Moncton*. Moncton: Régis Brun.

Charlebois v Moncton (City). 2001. 242 N.B.R. (2d) 259, 2001 NBCA 117.

City of Moncton. 2002. *Declaration of Official Bilingualism*, August 6. Moncton, New Brunswick: Moncton City Council.

_____. 2009. *Policy on Official Languages*, August. Moncton, New Brunswick: Moncton City Council. http://www.moncton.ca/Assets/ Government%20English/Policies/Policy%20on%20Official%20 Languages%202009.pdf [accessed on November 16, 2011].

Edelman, M. 1971. *Politics as Symbolic Action*. Chicago: Markham Publishing Company.

Griffiths, N. 2006. *From Migrant to Acadian*. Montreal and Kingston: McGill-Queen's University Press.

Jones v New Brunswick (Attorney General). 1975. 2 S.C.R. 182.

Landry, R, K. Deveau and R. Allard. 2006. "Langue publique et langue privée en milieu ethnolinguistique minoritaire : les relations avec le développement psycholangagier," *Francophonies d'Amérique*, 22: 167-184.

LeBlanc, B. 1996. "Tête à tête et charivari à Moncton : Rencontre interculturelle entre les Acadiens et les Anglophones de Moncton," *Les Cahiers de la Société Historique Acadienne*, 27: 4-17.

Pincombe, A. and E. Larracey. 1990. *Resurgo: The History of Moncton*. Moncton: City of Moncton.

Ottawa: One City, Two Languages Managing Municipal Services in English and French in Canada's Capital

Aaron Burry

In Canada, the City of Ottawa is a model when it comes to managing municipal services in English and French, the two official languages of Canada. This paper will seek to illustrate this by discussing three main themes:

- the city's bilingualism policy;
- the search for excellence in municipal services; and
- some of the procedures implemented by the city to promote the active offer of services in French, the language of the minority.

However, before getting to these themes, it is important to bring to light a few facts regarding the French language community in Ontario and in the Ottawa region.

The francophone community

Étienne Brûlé, who is recognized as the first Franco-Ontarian, set foot in Ontario in 1610, 400 years ago.

By the 19th century, at the inception of Bytown, which would later become Ottawa, a large French speaking community was already present in the region. In fact, the bilingual character of the city would be one of the factors in the decision to choose Ottawa as the capital of Canada.

In 1969, Canada passed the *Official Languages Act*, where English and French became the official languages of the country. The province of Ontario passed similar legislation in 1986, i.e., the *French Language Services Act* (1990), which enables Ontario municipalities, which are creations of the province, to legislate in the area of language of service.

Ottawa's francophones form a lively and vibrant community which, over the years, has created a network of French language institutions and organizations in all fields, including health, economics, arts and culture, education and social services. This represents great value-added for the City of Ottawa.

According to the 2006 Census, some 143,000 persons declared French as their mother tongue or as their first official language spoken (FOLS). This represents close to 18 percent of the total population. In addition, 39 percent of the city's total population (or 255,000 people) reported they spoke French.

Bilingualism policy

On May 9, 2001, some five months after the creation of the new City of Ottawa, the city adopted the *Bilingualism Policy* and the enabling bylaw (2001: 170).[6]

In essence, the *Bilingualism Policy*:

+ recognizes the equality of English and French speaking groups and citizens;
+ establishes the right of residents and municipal employees to choose, English or French, the language in which they wish to be served or to conduct business with the city;
+ designates bilingual positions to enable effective language-specific service delivery; and
+ defines the accountability of senior executives with respect to the management of services in both languages.

In 2006, the Ontario Superior Court issued a ruling on a legal action brought by the Canadians for Language Fairness, that the city's bilingualism policy did not violate any legal provisions. The court also ruled that the policy had been implemented in a reasonable, non-discriminatory and non-prejudicial way.

In January 2009, in response to two reports which presented a first assessment of the implementation of the *Bilingualism Policy*, city council and senior managers reiterated their commitment to delivering quality municipal services in English and in French to residents and visitors.

The first of these reports entitled *Feuille de route: Vers l'excellence dans l'application de la politique de bilinguisme de la Ville d'Ottawa* (Road Map: Towards Excellence in the Application of the City of Ottawa's Bilingualism Policy) by Praxis and Le Blanc (2007, also known as the Leblanc and Le Blanc Report) indicated that, according to researchers, the city's executives were quite unfamiliar with or had an incorrect understanding of the policy. The report proposed a dozen recommendations aimed at rectifying the

[6] The City of Ottawa was created on January 1, 2001 following an amalgamation of 12 governments, i.e., the Regional Municipality of Ottawa-Carleton and the 11 constituting municipalities, including the former City of Ottawa.

situation, accelerating implementation of the policy and improving the quality of services offered in French.

In particular, the consultants recommended:

+ a more sustained commitment from city executives, both elected officials and senior managers;
+ the proper understanding of the legal framework for the "equality of rights and privileges of both linguistic groups" in Canada; and
+ a better understanding of the specificities and needs of the francophone community.

The report also underlined that the French speaking community is becoming increasingly diversified in its ethnic and cultural make up.

The City's French Language Services Advisory Committee (FLSAC) presented the second report of 2009 to city council.[7] In addition to reiterating the consultants' recommendations, the FLSAC also presented several recommendations of its own, dealing with, in particular:

+ the promotion of the *Bilingualism Policy* among city employees;
+ actions to advance the organizational culture to make more room for bilingualism within the city apparatus;
+ better management and better coordination of French services, from program design to the assessment of their results;
+ the development of work plans by each of the city services to achieve excellence in providing service in both languages; and
+ the recruitment of more bilingual managers.

After these two reports were submitted, the city focused on a certain number of actions already undertaken to improve the delivery of services in French, including:

+ the designation of bilingual positions;
+ increased funding of day care services;
+ the improvement of recreational services in French;
+ the city's participation in various projects spearheaded by the francophone community; and
+ the tightening of instructions on bilingualism at public events and public consultations.

While reiterating its wish to do better, the city also committed to undertaking new actions to accelerate the implementation of the *Bilingualism Policy*.

---

[7] FLSAC is a group of volunteers made up of persons whose mother tongue is either English or French. Its mandate is to recommend to city council ways of accelerating the implementation of the bilingualism policy and improving services the city is to provide in both languages.

First of all, a bilingualism promotion campaign would be directed at City of Ottawa employees. The city also indicated that it would like to complete the designation of bilingual positions at all levels of the city structure. Finally, the city gave the go-ahead to one of the Advisory Committee's recommendations and committed to developing annual work plans for each of the city's departments that would include concrete actions to improve services in French. In so doing, the city once again recognized that both elected representatives and senior managers are responsible for the governance of English and French language services. Both of these entities must ensure that services are available, accessible and of comparable quality in both languages. This goes to the very definition of excellence *vis-à-vis* all services offered by the city.

Ottawa City Council again underlined the importance of the subject in 2007 when one of the 52 recommendations of its mid-mandate strategic plan underlined the fact that the city has two languages for the provision of services.

The search for excellence in municipal services

In 2008, the senior managers of the city defined "service excellence" as the primary goal of all city initiatives and undertakings in a document titled *"We see a City ..."* While this document makes no direct reference to language, it should be understood that bilingualism will be brought to bear in the active offering of all "excellent" municipal services. This approach of service excellence will also govern the management of all city programs and projects, such as:

+ the design of a master plan for recreational services, to include improved services in French;
+ an update of the city's cultural and artistic policy; and
+ the provision of bilingual services in all city partnerships, such as the redevelopment of Lansdowne Park in cooperation with the private sector.

Moreover, two entities, FLSAC and the French Language Services Division (FLSD), were officially given a mandate to monitor the management and governance of bilingualism in the city and recommend actions likely to improve the delivery of services in French. Made up of volunteers, the FLSAC has a mandate to advise the city on bilingualism and services in French. For example, here are just a few cases the committee turned its attention to in recent years:

+ the reform of the municipal governance structure;
+ city budgets and their impact on the city's ability to meet its commitments regarding the two languages of service;
+ the funding of francophone organizations;
+ bilingualism in public transit;
+ the creation of a public health council; and
+ the opening of the Shenkman Arts Centre in Orleans.

The French Language Services Division answers directly to the city manager, the city's highest ranking employee. The four employees in this division mainly serve as a resource to and offer their unique expertise to the city's various departments. The FLSD is also responsible for the city's translation services and the management of complaints regarding services in French.

Mechanisms aimed at promoting the active offer of services in both languages

One of the most effective means of managing services in both languages has proven to be the designation of bilingual positions.

The *Bilingualism Policy* states that the city shall designate a certain number of positions as requiring skills in both languages. For example, the policy designates all upper echelon positions from levels one through three to be bilingual; this is to ensure that senior managers are able to act as spokespeople for the city, while exemplifying leadership in bilingualism for all staff.

The policy also requires that positions at all other levels within the organization be reviewed and that some be appropriately designated to enable the city to effectively offer services in both languages. In June 2008, the city completed the Bilingualism Position Designation Project. This was an ambitious undertaking where all of the city's positions were evaluated to determine which ones would require the knowledge of both languages. This project, which was spearheaded by the FLSD and the Human Resources Department, was completed with the cooperation of all of the city's work units.

Since July 1, 2008, the city has been practicing what has come to be called "continuous designation". Like the Designation Project, the purpose of this procedure is to ensure that the city can continue to rely on enough qualified staff to provide quality services in both languages at all times.

In late 2009, 16 percent of all of the city's positions had received one of two designations:

- "designated day-one ready" positions requiring the candidates to meet the language requirements immediately on taking the position; or
- for "designated bilingual" position, a candidate commits to achieving the language requirements of the position by taking language training offered to city employees.

In addition to the designation of bilingual positions, Ottawa has chosen to resort to other ways of promoting the establishment of services in both languages. The *Bilingualism Policy* compels each of the city's departments to produce a work plan each year to improve French language services. These plans must be submitted to city council for approval and be the subject of an annual report. This policy requirement should be applied for the first time in 2010.

The city deploys other mechanisms and procedures to promote the offer of services of comparable quality in both languages. Each year, the city offers its employees, particularly those occupying designated positions, an opportunity to improve their second language skills. Various formats are offered to meet the learners' needs: group sessions, individual tutoring, training in the workplace and computer-assisted training. At all times, an average of 250 city employees take four hours of language training per week. The learners' success and satisfaction rates are very high.

The city also offers its employees a number of opportunities for professional training in French. The goal of this training is multifaceted:

- it allows francophones to take training in their mother tongue;
- it allows anglophones to further their knowledge of French, in a context other than a second language course; and
- it exemplifies the city's commitment to enabling staff to work in the official language of their choice.

The city's translation service offers a variety of linguistic services in both English and French. It handles an average of 70 requests per business day, for a total of close to six million words or roughly 17,000 pages of text annually. In recent years, the city has undertaken several initiatives to further improve its linguistic services, such as the development of protocols for urgent translations from Ottawa Public Health, including messages required during the massive H1N1 vaccination campaign in the fall of 2009.

In 2009, the city launched a promotional campaign intended for its employees, the purpose of which was to create more awareness of the

Bilingualism Policy. This gave rise to the "Une Ville, deux langues / One City, two languages" campaign. The slogan of this campaign and its visual signature, a stylized flower combining Ontario's trillium and the *fleur-de-lys de la Francophonie*, were designed following discussion groups that brought together the city's employees. The campaign mainly involved the distribution of promotional items and presentations to groups of city employees.

Finally, a few events are held at city hall to promote bilingualism. For example, the Mayor's *Rendez-vous francophone* which, over the years, has become a must-attend event for the francophone community. Every September 25, the Franco-Ontarian Flag Day is attended by more than 700 children from schools near city hall.

More importantly, each day, the City of Ottawa offers a myriad of widely ranging services in either official language. It would be impossible to provide a complete list of services in French provided by the city, but the following provides a few examples.

Since 2007, the city has been implementing a catch-up plan for subsidized child care services in French. As of last year, parity of funding for English and French language services had been reached. At the outset, approximately 11 percent of the city's expenditures went towards French language services. Today, more than 16 percent of subsidies go to these services, which is in line with the demographic proportion of francophone children.

At the Parks, Recreation and Cultural Services Department, the number of activities offered in French has continued to increase since 2005. Several new initiatives have also been developed to promote these services and to recruit bilingual staff. As a result, registration revenues for French language activities have increased by 117 percent between 2005 and 2009, a fact that is not lost on the city treasurer.

A third example is the recent opening of the Shenkman Arts Centre in Orleans. Since last fall, the centre has been offering a wide array of French language artistic courses and performances, in keeping with its client base.

Over the years, city procedures regarding bilingualism at public events and community consultations have not always been followed. The city manager recently reminded those concerned of the city's practices and strengthened the monitoring of these procedures.

Active offer and comparable services

The City of Ottawa's *Bilingualism Policy* is based on two important pillars, i.e.
  + the notion of an active offer; and
  + the concept of providing services of comparable quality in either official language.

The notion of an active offer consists of a series of measures and actions undertaken by the city to clearly indicate to clients that city services are available and accessible in both official languages. They can then decide which language to use with no fear of undue delays. The city is then required to ensure, for example, that:
  + documents and posters are clearly visible in both languages;
  + at least one bilingual person is present at all times at the various city counters;
  + all employees, regardless of their linguistic capabilities, greet clients in both official languages; and
  + during public events or consultations, the facilitator or the emcee clearly indicates the measures the city has put in place to ensure service in both languages.

Though these practices seem quite straightforward, they do require that quality control mechanisms are in place at all times and that persons responsible for application of the language policies have been identified.

When the city seeks to offer services of comparable quality, it not only recognizes the equality of both language groups, but also the fact that these groups have different social structures and dynamics. Municipal services need to be designed in such a way as to meet the varying needs of different communities. In other words, a service in one language is not necessarily a carbon copy of a service offered in the other language. Here is an example: For the last several years, the two local French language school boards have been more active in setting up child care programs for pre-schoolers and after-four activities for students than their English language counterparts. In the spirit of the *Bilingualism Policy*, the city sought means of enhancing the actions of the French school boards. As a result, joint programs with those boards are quite different than those developed in partnership with the English language boards.

Another example would be public health and public transit campaigns. Rarely does a translated slogan or, for that matter, a marketing strategy work well for both linguistic groups. The better way to go is to develop culturally sensitive campaigns and programs of comparable quality.

Conclusion

This paper is intended to show that Ottawa is, in Canada, a model when it comes to the delivery of municipal services in both languages. Nonetheless, some challenges still lie ahead for the city when it comes to achieving its objective of providing accessible services of comparable quality in English and French. It is a complex process which hinges on contributions by numerous public servants on a day-to-day basis.

As indicated earlier, the city will have to take the means necessary to further develop its organizational culture in order to assign more importance to the planning, design and delivery of services to the francophone minority. As is all too often the case, bilingualism is not given enough weight right from the start of planning processes. In order for this to materialize and in keeping with the recommendations arising from the first evaluation of the implementation of the *Bilingualism Policy*, more sustained commitment on the part of elected officials and senior managers is needed. In the same vein, action is required to improve both the recruitment and retention of bilingual staff.

The city has everything to gain by putting in place various mechanisms to ensure ongoing and productive dialogue with the francophone community. Among other things, this would be a way of acknowledging the contributions this community has made over the years and is still making. The city will have to take into account the changing nature of the francophone community. The presence of and contributions by francophone racial and ethnic minorities are becoming increasingly evident – a factor that should influence the design and delivery of services in French.

Finally, Ottawa must periodically take stock of all of the actions it has taken to implement its *Bilingualism Policy*. This will enable it to make adjustments and to come up with new ways of improving things.

References

City of Ottawa. 2001. *Bilingualism Policy* and the enabling bylaw. Retrieved from: http://ottawa.ca/city_hall/french_services/bilingualismpolicy_en.html.

_____. 2008. *We see a City ...* Unpublished document.

_____. 2010. *Mid-mandate strategic plan 2007-2010*. Retrieved from: http://ottawa.ca/city_hall/corporate_plan/plan/strategic_plan_en.pdf.

FLSAC. 2009. *Second Report of 2009.* Retrieved from: http://www.ottawa. ca/calendar/ottawa/citycouncil/csedc/2009/01-20/01%20-%20 ACS2008-CCV-FLS-0002-fre.htm.

Government of Canada. 1969. *Official Languages Act.* Retrieved from: http://laws-lois.justice.gc.ca/eng/acts/O-3.01/.

Government of Ontario. 1990. *French Language Services Act.* Retrieved from: http://www.e-laws.gov.on.ca/html/statutes/english/elaws_ statutes_90f32_e.htm.

Leblanc, P. and J.-C. Le Blanc. 2007. *Feuille de route – Vers l'excellence dans l'application de la Politique de bilinguisme de la Ville d'Ottawa* (Road Map: Towards Excellence in the Application of the City of Ottawa's Bilingualism Policy). Report submitted to the French Language Services Branch of the City of Ottawa, Ottawa, Canada. Retrieved from: http://pdf.cyberpresse.ca/ledroit/rapportleblanc.pdf.

The City of Ottawa: Symbolic Representation and Public Image

Caroline Andrew and Guy Chiasson

Introduction

The City of Ottawa is located in the centre of the national capital region (NCR) and has a population of approximately 900,000 (812,129 according to the 2006 Census). The NCR links the province of Ontario with the City of Gatineau and neighbouring municipalities in the province of Quebec, and had a population of 1,130,761 in 2006. According to the 2006 Census, 17.7 percent of the population in Ottawa had French as either its first language or its first official language spoken (FOLS), and 39 percent of Ottawa citizens spoke French.

The purpose of this chapter is to present an overview of the City of Ottawa's symbolic representation of itself with respect to language planning. The discussion below is divided into four sections: past relations between the Government of Canada and the City of Ottawa; recent organizational changes to the city; the city's main means of implementing language planning; and current challenges and opportunities. The main focus is on the municipal government, as opposed to language relations in civil society and the education system. The goal is to illustrate language planning as it is handled within the municipal government.

A step back in time

The symbolic representation and public image of the City of Ottawa cannot be understood without referring to its historical background. As suggested below, the City of Ottawa has trouble seeing and representing itself as a national capital. That difficulty stems from the past relationship between the Government of Canada and the City of Ottawa. Understanding the dynamics of that relationship will make it possible to gain a better grasp of changes in the symbolic representation of the city and the impact on its approach to official languages.

Ottawa was chosen as the capital of Canada in 1857, following a period in which the capital had moved between Montreal, Kingston, Toronto and Quebec City. It was not until after World War II and the postwar period that the federal public service began to experience steady growth. However, the role of the federal government in local affairs dates back to an earlier time. The federal government started to involve itself directly in municipal affairs in 1899, with the creation of the Ottawa Improvement Commission. The name is telling: the City of Ottawa needed improvement, and the federal government was going to take charge of it. The city, under the circumstances, was therefore in a relationship of dependence. While it is true that the city accepted "gifts" (parks, the Rideau Canal, bike paths) from the federal government, it did not incorporate them into its definition of self. For a long time, the reaction of the city was to view itself as the government of the local residents, responsible only for the delivery of basic services (streets, sidewalks, firefighters, police), and not at all involved in spending on "luxuries" (parks, public spaces, planning), much of which fell under the jurisdiction of the federal government, by means of the National Capital Commission (NCC), which replaced the Ottawa Improvement Commission. Therefore, the city increasingly adopted its image of serving local residents and having no duty to represent all Canadians.

Furthermore, the City of Ottawa was at the service of the business elite, which quickly became predominantly anglophone, and paid little attention to the francophone population. The city's bilingual image was therefore relatively weak. Anglophones gradually forgot the significant role played by francophones in the founding and growth of the city (for example, the creation of the General Hospital and the University of Ottawa). The 2001 municipal amalgamation limited French-language services (both in quantity and in quality) to regions that were historically francophone, while slightly increasing French-language services in the west end of the new city. Amalgamation was carried out without taking into account Ottawa's role as the capital of Canada; instead, the city was merely an administrative entity that reduced services to a common denominator.[8]

Recent changes to the City of Ottawa: service excellence

Following the municipal amalgamation, with everyone governed by the same political entity, disputes broke out between rural, suburban and urban areas of the city. As well, each budget period gave rise to disputes between

---

[8] Note that the amalgamation took place when a highly neo-liberal provincial government was in power, and it therefore aimed explicitly to reduce services and taxes.

constituents who wanted reductions in services and taxes, and constituents who feared reductions in services and wanted increased action by the city to meet new needs.

That backdrop of conflict is important, since it is the context in which the City of Ottawa decided to launch the Service Excellence Plan, which was intended to be a strategy to reorganize services with a focus on the quality of response to the needs of the public. The idea of service excellence will satisfy those who criticize the city for overspending as well as those who criticize the city for not acting to meet new needs. The goal here is to see how the Service Excellence Plan made it possible to reframe the issue of language planning. The city expressed a desire to be a preferred employer, broadening the definition of excellence to include highly qualified staff and an image of a leading-edge city. Obviously, the term "excellence" can mean many things but, in speeches of the city, the themes of fairness and inclusion kept appearing with (of course) the themes of effectiveness and efficiency. As a City of Ottawa strategy, the purpose of the Service Excellence Plan was not to improve the city's performance as the national capital. It was a 'municipal' strategy to improve public service delivery rather than a strategy to better represent a Canadian national identity. However, in spite of that, the Service Excellence Plan has had a significant impact on the functioning of the city as a capital city.

With the Service Excellence Plan, the City of Ottawa is trying to show a new attitude as a government, competing with other employers, including the federal government, to be an employer of choice. The city's definition of excellence is broad, which paves the way for a new representation of the city, especially with regard to the importance the city intends to give to the two languages of service. That intention stems largely from competition between cities in an era of globalization and an increasing need to be positioned as a welcoming community, using every asset to create an identity.

The City of Ottawa has already used the themes of nature and leading-edge technology to create an identity but now, with the problems in the high technology industry and nature alone not being a sufficiently unique theme to define Ottawa, the city must include other aspects in its symbolic representation. To project an image of excellence, key themes are ones that build on the history and traditions specific to the city, which celebrate diversity and harmonious co-existence. Those themes reflect increased attention to the bilingual aspect of the city and the ability to provide high quality French-language services. That is why the Service Excellence Plan is a potential opportunity – with an emphasis on "potential" – for the city to adopt explicit language planning practices. The next section looks at the means available to the City of Ottawa to implement its policy on bilingualism.

The rationale behind the current means of implementing the Bilingualism Policy

Ottawa city councillors enacted the *Bilingualism Policy* in 2001. The policy reaffirms the commitment of the City of Ottawa to provide services to employees and the public in both official languages. The policy is largely based on the policy of the former City of Ottawa. Specific provisions of the *Bilingualism Policy* govern a number of areas in the municipal government, in particular, communications and the active offer of services to the public in both languages. As for government employees, the *Bilingualism Policy* provides for the organization of work that includes designated bilingual positions, language training and cultural program management (CAWI and City of Ottawa 2010).

The *Bilingualism Policy* provides for two main means of implementation, namely, the designation of bilingual positions and the creation of annual work plans for the various services of the city. The initial designation of bilingual positions has been completed and the creation of annual work plans is in progress. Rather than creating separate plans for French-language services, the possibility of including French-language service planning in a more general process is now being discussed. This will be a significant challenge, but also a key opportunity to entrench French-language services as a regular part of the city's services.

The goal here is not to describe the means of implementation in detail, but instead to focus on the underlying rationale. The rationale that connects the two means is the inextricable link between relationships within the municipal government (internal) and relationships with the outside (external). The designation of bilingual positions implies the recruitment of government employees who can deliver high quality services in French and therefore do annual work planning to expand French-language services. To the extent that internal planning is effective, transparent and inclusive (which implies the involvement of community groups and organizations), the outcome of the planning will be good external relations. Without the designation of bilingual positions, the ability to plan effectively would be limited, since there would not be staff members in place who could arrange for French-language service planning or provide French-language services that meet the needs of the community.

That inextricable link between internal and external relationships is crucial to the successful implementation of the *Bilingualism Policy*. Planning currently involves community participation or partnerships. To successfully create a planning process with the community requires two things: leadership from the city's senior management and the involvement of government employees who have the expertise, means and support from superiors necessary to design new French-language services reflecting the development of the city and its linguistic communities. Those two things can be achieved by designating bilingual positions, planning services, and then connecting with civil society organizations. Often, institutions focus on public services and fail to realize that external success is impossible without internal means. The City of Ottawa therefore has potential means, through the designation of bilingual positions and creation of annual work plans, to increase bilingualism and the importance of the francophone community in its symbolic representation and public image.

A key role in implementing a strategy to strengthen ties with the francophone community is played by the French Language Services Branch (FLSB), which is in charge of implementing the *Bilingualism Policy* and which, as of recently, reports directly to the senior management of the city. The City of Ottawa currently receives a grant from the Ministry of Canadian Heritage to incorporate new practices in the city's everyday operations. The grant has been used mainly to increase the ability of the francophone community organizations to fulfill their mandates, as well as to put pressure on the City of Ottawa. The community thereby gains the ability to maintain effective ties with the city and change one-time requests into ongoing interaction. That investment in community capacity will institutionalize the ties between the city and the francophone community.

The FLSB has also sought to increase the number of fields of activity in which there is interaction between francophone groups and the city. In addition to groups already having ties with the city, such as *Regroupement des gens d'affaires* (RGA), the FLSB has established relationships with organizations providing French-language services to the homeless and organizations providing services to francophone immigrants. That strategy has a number of benefits. For example, new fields of activity in the city are affected by requirements for sector-specific French-language services. As well, various organizing principles, such as equal funding of agencies, a service resulting from the decentralization of Government of Ontario services, a service associated with a high priority program of the city to improve French-language services, may be studied and tested. Lastly, new organizations that involve other parts of the francophone community may start to interact with the city. That is important because the City of Ottawa, like any other similar organization, is responsive to the entire population as well, of course, to the representation of the usual spokespersons. Helping new groups interact with the city makes those groups aware of the importance of the city for the creation of services tailored to their needs and makes the city aware of the vast array of groups that require proper French-language services.

In short, the FLSB has used the federal government grant to increase its interactions in various fields of activity in which francophone community organizations and the city are involved. That work is moving toward institutionalizing those interactions and incorporating them into the city's everyday operations. Of course, it is not only the FLSB that is initiating interaction between the city and francophone communities. One example involves the Service Excellence Plan Implementation Office and the Human Resources Department. Those two units worked with the community group City for All Women Initiative (CAWI) to create the "Equity and Inclusion Lens" to educate city employees so that they interact more positively with marginalized groups. It should be noted that that does not replace the specific provisions for various groups, such as the *Bilingualism Policy* for francophones. However, it makes it easier for city staff to develop inclusive and collaborative practices with community groups.

In this analysis of the rationale underlying the *Bilingualism Policy*, another means of community participation should be mentioned, namely, the French Language Services Advisory Committee. After the municipal amalgamation, the new City of Ottawa created a series of advisory committees, including the French Language Services Advisory Committee. The composition of the committee was specified from the start to be half francophone and half anglophone. The French Language Services Advisory Committee has worked on various issues, including the services of the Ottawa Public Library, child care services and funding for *Centre Espoir Sophie*. In addition, the committee has monitored and supported the work of the FLSB.

The advisory committees have failed to reach their full potential for lack of management and political support. The city has not given them resources (other than parking expenses for meetings); therefore, their ability to delve into issues and conduct research has been extremely limited.

Moving forward: challenges and opportunities

This chapter is based on the potential represented by the link between the Service Excellence Plan and the existing means for implementing the *Bilingualism Policy*. While the project can be viewed optimistically as a path toward a city representing itself as bilingual and providing services consistent with that representation, major challenges must be kept in mind.

First, the City of Ottawa's corporate culture must change so that the importance of French-language services is recognized to a greater extent. As well, it must be recognized that changing corporate culture is difficult in times of budgetary restraint and that now is definitely such a time. It is important to take action immediately to lay the groundwork, and then acknowledge that it will take some time to apply the policies. Getting off to a good start is important for a long-term change in corporate culture; successfully introducing the creation of annual work plans for the development of French-language services would be a good example of "getting off to a good start".

A second challenge is to raise the profile and increase the visibility of francophones. It is essential that the city include a francophone component in all public events. That effort would also help change the corporate culture and embody the new definition of excellence that the City of Ottawa wants to create.

The third challenge comes back to the issue of management, political leadership and commitment for the implementation of the *Bilingualism Policy*. The report by Leblanc and Le Blanc (2007) is pessimistic, stating that the City of Ottawa does not show firm political commitment to bilingualism. It is clear that champions will be required, especially in the upper levels of the municipal government, for the policy to succeed.

It must be noted that there are best practices at the City of Ottawa that illustrate the close links between the internal and the external, and those practices can be used as examples in other areas. Two examples are amendments to the policy for the child care needs of francophone immigrants and French-language recreational services. The development of French-language child care is the result of a partnership between city staff (the Child Care Branch and the FLSB) and the community (organizations representing the child care community, the francophone community and the French Language Services Advisory Committee), as well as the expertise of an external consultant. The outcome has been an increase in French-language child care services, and services to meet the needs of francophone immigrants. Immigrants, many of whom work night shifts, cannot make much use of public child-care facilities, which are open from 9 a.m. to 6 p.m. French-language home-based child care services therefore had to be developed. Two successes were achieved: increased services and services tailored to new needs.

French-language recreational services are also the result of close collaboration between city staff, proactively developing French-language services, and francophone community groups and associations. The City of Ottawa, in cooperation with the community, set up an advertising campaign for French-language recreational services, to inform the francophone community about existing services. The collaboration with the community has increased the dissemination of information and bolstered the campaign's success.

Conclusion

To conclude, let us return to the main issue for the second theme of the symposium, namely, symbolic representation and public image. It was argued above that the City of Ottawa has trouble seeing itself – and therefore representing itself – as the capital of a bilingual country. However, there are now two series of initiatives that may lead to new perspectives: first, the start of the implementation of the *Bilingualism Policy* by designating bilingual positions and creating annual work plans and, second, the City of Ottawa's Service Excellence Plan. By building on best practices, the two initiatives, despite the challenges, may result in a symbolic representation and public image of the city that better reflects the bilingualism and the contribution of the francophone community that characterize life in Ottawa.

References

City for All Women Initiative (CAWI) and City of Ottawa. 2010. *Equity and Inclusion Lens. Diversity Snapshot: Francophones*. Ottawa: CAWI.

Leblanc, P. and J.-C. Le Blanc. 2007. *Feuille de route : Vers l'excellence dans l'application de la Politique de bilinguisme de la Ville d'Ottawa*. Report submitted to the French Language Services Branch of the City of Ottawa, Ottawa, Canada. Retrieved from: http://pdf.cyberpresse.ca/ledroit/rapportleblanc.pdf.

A Nation of Two Official Languages: Helsinki as Helsingfors

Maria Björnberg-Enckell

Finland, in Finnish *Suomi*, is situated between Sweden and Russia, as a border-country between the East and the West, in the north-eastern corner of the European Union. The country gained its independence in 1917 as an officially bilingual nation with Finnish and Swedish as the national languages, and Helsinki, in Swedish *Helsingfors*, as its capital.

In the following chapter, I will concentrate on what the status of national language means for the minority-speakers, the Swedish, in the officially bilingual capital. The focus will be administration and education because schools are strategic for the future of any society, and especially so for a minority. When, for example, the indigenous people of Finland, the *Sami*, did not get education in their own language at school, their language and traditions were randomly passed to only some children, not to all.

The necessity of education is well understood. Basic, as well as secondary and higher education, is provided in Swedish in the capital and in the parts of Finland where the language is spoken because Swedish is protected by the constitution. There are now constant demands to make the language a voluntary subject and even questions about the bilingual status of the nation. Until recently, no political party had been pursuing these goals. Now members of the *Party Perussuomalaiset* (Finnish Popular Party) have given voice to these ideas. The Association of Finnish Culture and Identity, originally founded in 1906, supports the unilingual nation as its central proposition and actively works to promote it (Association of Finnish Culture and Identity 2010). In addition, the relatively new xenophobic tendencies, growing with the number of foreigners living in Finland, have found a political home.

Having lost a political conflict about the orientation of North Ostrobotnia towards southern Vaasa instead of northern Oulu because of the constitutionally defined language rights of the Swedish, newly elected Prime Minister Mari Kiviniemi (*Centerparty*) stated that she has difficulty standing behind the mandatory learning of Swedish in the schools (Hufvudstadsbladet 2010). It is obvious that economic and ecological threats have influenced the political climate. Attitudes towards the Swedish language have been cooling over the last few years. It is also evident that the Swedish-speaking minority are ultimately dependent on the political measures taken by the Finnish majority and the political leadership.

The capital of Finland

Helsinki/Helsingfors is a "pocket-size" metropolis of some 580,000 inhabitants. The official city website enables a choice between six languages on its front page: Finnish, Swedish, English, German, French and Russian (City of Helsinki 2010a). For approximately six hundred years as the eastern part of the Swedish Kingdom, Swedish was the first administrative language of the country. The population on the coastline, those living in the archipelago and in the cities mostly spoke Swedish, whereas the majority of the people were Finnish-speakers. German was widely used by merchants and intellectuals, as was French, Latin and Russian. Becoming an autonomous Grand Duchy, as part of the Russian Empire in 1809, Helsingfors was established as the capital in 1812, instead of former Åbo (Ibid.).

The Russian language gained influence and was certainly required for those aspiring to a career in the Russian empire, although the administration in Finland continued in Swedish. Towards the end of the 19th century, the majority language, Finnish, was strengthened, first, as an educational language at primary schools and later as an administrative language. Books written in Finnish began to appear by the mid-19th century.[9] As independence from Russia was acquired in 1917, the first *Language Act of Finland* was passed in 1922, giving equal status to Finnish and Swedish, the two national languages.

In January 2004, the old act was replaced by a new act that also focussed on the constitutionally determined national languages, granting both groups the right to use their language on an equal basis. National institutions are bilingual, but other authorities and municipalities are either unilingual or bilingual, depending on the size of the minority (Finlex 2003). Historically, Helsinki, as well as the coastline to the east and to the west, had a large Swedish population. It was a city of many languages. As a result of the law and according to the size of its Swedish minority, it is today a formally bilingual city. Recently, English has gained much influence, such that the city can be called trilingual, or where Swedish is forgotten, bilingual in Finnish and English.

[9] The national epos by Elias Lönnroth, *Kalevala*, was published in 1849.

Language planning

The *Language Act of Finland*, defining two national languages, determines that although a minority-language, Swedish is not defined as such. This provision creates many opportunities as well as many difficulties. Different institutions on national, regional and municipal levels carry out administrative planning. The national authority evaluating the observance of the *Language Act* is the Ministry of Justice. The Advisory Board on Language Affairs set by the government is a wide-based body of experts representing various sectors of society. The *Report of the Government on the application of language legislation 2009* (Ministry of Justice 2010) should be considered a tool for monitoring the implementation of the *Language Act*, as well as a description of the linguistic conditions of Finland. Language planning is not required, but recommended, for municipalities and cities. As these are either defined as unilingual or multilingual, the linguistic regulations vary throughout the country.

The city council is the highest decision-making body of Helsinki/ Helsingfors. The council determines important financial matters such as the budget and the municipal part of the income tax.[10] The municipal tax brings in roughly half of the budget and is collected to cover the municipal costs of education, health care and social welfare, all provided to the citizens for free, or at a very modest fee. These municipal services, including day care (there is a right to childcare for all children), consume about 75 percent of the budget and are partly financed by the government.

The languages used at council meetings are Finnish or Swedish and councilors are free to choose their preferred language. For those with political aspirations, some fluency in both languages is required, particularly of the Swedish minority-speakers. The chairman of the city council addresses the meeting in both languages, but longer speeches are often only in Finnish.[11] Helsinki has no administrative responsibility for overall language planning, however, strategic papers about the needs for municipal services to the Swedish-speaking population have been prepared. City departments act on the basis of administrative or political initiative. Translations are produced by various departments with varying frequency and there is a great deal of variety in the actual language practices.

The only Swedish divisions of the city are the Swedish Education Division in the Department of Education, the Swedish Adult Education

---

[10] The municipal tax in 2010 was at 17.5% and at 18.5% in 2011.
[11] All meetings are webcast on http://www.helsinkikanava.fi/.

Centre Arbis and the Swedish Division in the Social Service Department. Swedish schools, day care centres, as well as pre-schools constitute a network of institutions covering the city. For Swedish-speaking children, as well as for the bilingual children using two languages at home, these institutions are vital both for their Swedish-language skills, and their cultural and linguistic identity. The educational path from day care centre to pre-school, contemporary school, high school and vocational or university studies can be followed in Swedish. Swedish day care and primary schools are situated around the city, but they are concentrated in the central, western and southern parts where the Swedish population is more dense.

Departments such as the Department of Culture, Sports, Youth, etc. ... do not have separate Swedish administrative bodies, and the Swedish-speaking civil servants delivering Swedish services are part of a bilingual department. Language practices tend to vary depending on the attitude held by the management of the department towards the Swedish-speaking minority.

Enhancing equality and quality in education

Since the reforms in 1970-77, Finland has emphasized equality in education through the founding of the nine-year long comprehensive school system. Today, not only primary, but also secondary, as well as higher education, are provided free of charge.[12] Basic, as well as higher education, is provided in separate Finnish or Swedish language schools. The University of Helsinki, as well as some other universities are bilingual, but teaching is delivered mostly in either Finnish or Swedish language institutions. Organizing primary and secondary education is a municipal, not federal government responsibility, although financing is partly the responsibility of the federal state.

The 11 member educational committee always has two Swedish representatives, and the committee is divided into Finnish and Swedish divisions. The divisions decide on matters concerning the location of the schools and they are responsible for securing their cultural independence. All schools in the capital have individual elected boards consisting of parents, teachers and other personnel and, at upper secondary schools, students also sit on the boards (City of Helsinki 2010b).

Although education is free and most schools are public, the achievements of the students seem to be high, compared to other countries reported in

---

[12] There are five foreign language schools operating in Helsinki, some of which are charging a tuition fee.

the OECD program for international student assessment. The 15-year-olds were ranked the best or close to the best in mathematics, scientific studies and reading skills of the PISA 2000, 2003 and 2006 studies (Centre for Educational Assesment, University of Helsinki 2006). These overall results in a sparsely populated country indicate that students are provided with good education regardless of how big or small the city, how remote the school or whether it is a Finnish or a Swedish school. Special education is easily accessible and provided for approximately 10 percent of students in comprehensive schools and upper secondary schools. The focus is placed on the ones lagging behind, and streaming students into vocational and upper secondary school is not done before the age of 16. In Helsinki/Helsingfors, forty different native languages are taught to immigrant children.

All children in Finland study a minimum of two languages other than their first language (mother tongue), one of these languages being the other national language. In Finnish schools, education in English usually starts in Grade 3 or 4 and in Swedish in Grade 7. In Swedish schools, education in Finnish starts in Grade 3, and the other language (usually English) in Grade 5. Since 2005, the "other" national language is no longer a mandatory subject for the matriculation exams.

Swedish immersion was introduced in Finland in the late 1980s, using the Canadian model. Immersion in Helsinki is conducted in the minority language, Swedish, not vice versa. It starts in preschool at the age of 3-6 continuing through to Grade 9 of comprehensive school. Every year, a few immersion students in Grade 7 apply and are accepted to attend Swedish schools. In Helsinki, Finnish children in Swedish immersion make up to a third of the amount of children attending Swedish schools.

Research at Vaasa University in Finland by Siv Björklund shows that the immersion pupils master their first and second languages (Finnish or Swedish), a third and even a fourth language very well, even better than non-immersion students. Immersion students also become more confident about their ability to learn languages, more advanced in their use of English and more open to learning new languages. Bilingualism seems to promote the acquisition of a third and a fourth language; and languages seem generally more easily acquired by bilingual children (Björklund & Suni 2000). A challenge for the immersion program in the city is to establish well functioning pathways from day care to school in order to guarantee sufficient and evenly distributed numbers of students in the immersion classes. Immersion at day care is usually required in order for a child to go to immersion classes at 7 years of age. Day care institutions and schools are, however, administered by different departments of the city. This creates a risk of uncoordinated planning leading to the path through immersion day care to immersion schools not being easily accessible for families. This might result in smaller numbers of children in the immersion systems and fewer immersion classes.

Language practices

At birth, the mother tongue of a child is registered as either Finnish, Swedish or other; there is no option to register the child as a bilingual individual. The mother tongue status indicates the language that authorities will use for contact and also what the educational language will be. The status can later be changed. In Helsinki, bilingual families are common and children grow up speaking two languages at home, Swedish with mother and Finnish with father, or vice versa. Parents are also by law granted the right to choose the language of education for their children. Traditionally, children of bilingual families attend Swedish school and study in the minority language. This trend leads to difficulties in the forecasting of numbers of pupils at Swedish schools since the bilingual children who registered as Finnish speakers (mother's first language) attend Swedish school. In February 2010, there were 13 percent more children registered for the first grade in Swedish schools than there were Swedish speaking 7-year olds, according to the population register. Children with a Finnish parent are, throughout their education at Swedish schools, taught Finnish at a mother tongue level, whereas children from unilingual, Swedish homes attend beginner's courses for Finnish.

In Swedish-language schools, the percentage of children coming from bilingual families is high; however, not all parents of children choose to speak Swedish in their contacts with the school, but prefer to use their own language. Finnish is also strongly present outside the classroom, during breaks and in discussions between pupils. Interestingly enough, even if a pupil speaks more Finnish at home, attending Swedish school seems to strengthen the Swedish identity of the child and most students will then take their further studies also in Swedish. When marrying a Finnish-speaker, the bilingual person graduating from a Swedish school might speak Swedish to his or her child even if Finnish is the language used with his or her spouse. The social network established during school is enduring and, regardless of traditions at home, the child will be exposed to Swedish culture. Thus, Swedish school seems to have a very strong impact on the definition of identity and the understanding of the self as part of the minority or as a bilingual person (Kovero and Londen 2009).

54

The private sector and the civic society are considered important providers for Swedish service. Day care centres, preschools and homes for elderly are operated by several old societies on a non-profit basis. Institutions founded more than a century ago to promote general health, child care or culture are still operating. Foundations promoting the Swedish culture and language in Finland continue to support artists and writers of today. The Swedish Cultural Foundation, developed to support cultural and educational aspirations, is one of the biggest. The Swedish theatre in the centre of town, as well as other commercial institutions, are clearly visible in the city.

As well, the Luckan Finnish-Swedish Information Centre is centrally situated and a well-known provider of tickets and childrens' books, as well as general information on events and functions. Recently an information centre for immigrants and foreigners has been opened. Coordination and language planning for services such as web services for the youth, is being handled in the back office of Luckan. Free use of the Internet and computers, as well as Swedish newspapers and magazines, theatre and readings for children in addition to sales of tickets to Swedish cultural programs create a steady flow of visitors of all ages.

Language evaluation, challenges and suggestions

The Advisory Board on Language Affairs suggests that, in political decision-making and legislative work, it is important to evaluate the influence of each decision on the possibilities to secure linguistic rights. The board suggests an assessment of linguistic rights and how these rights will be safeguarded when administrative changes are made or when organizational functions and tasks are redefined. The board also suggests the incorporation of compliance with the language legislation and evaluation of how planned solutions will promote the use of both national languages in the manner required by the *Language Act* (Ministry of Justice 2009). Structural reforms of authorities at the municipal and regional levels may lead to bigger units, and in these new authorities, the Swedish perspective might clearly be diminished and more easily forgotten. The recent political decision regarding the regional orientation of the Kokkola/Karleby area towards Swedish southern Vaasa/Vasa indicates the strength of language rights in shaping the political map.

In a recent report, the Audit Committee of Helsinki suggests that all departments should prepare a plan for Swedish services and that they also should evaluate their capacity for implementation. It argues that the Department of Human Resources should evaluate whether Swedish-language courses have been sufficient and offered frequently enough. The committee also suggests that evaluation should also be conducted on how Swedish-language skills have developed since 2004 (Tarkastuslautakunta [Audit Committee] 2007).

Coordination of Swedish language services becomes quite a challenge since there is no director responsible for the minority-language issues which are handled in different departments. It is obvious that clear responsibility for language planning in the different administrations and on different levels of administration is required for effectiveness. The Taxell Paradox makes the point that bilingual institutions tend to lead to a unilingual environment in the majority language, Finnish, whereas unilingual Swedish institutions support national bilingualism by nurturing the Swedish language. Nonetheless, it is difficult to explain to majority-speakers that Swedish, not bilingual, schools are a necessity for the survival of the language or that, more generally, solutions demanded for the minority might be different from the solutions for the majority.

A scenario report by *Kuntaliitto* (the Association of Finnish Local and Regional Authorities) and the Think Tank Magma, presents recommendations for the future in the publication entitled *Swedish Finland 2030*. The report emphasizes the need for high quality education and good services for children. It suggests that Finland needs a national language strategy addressing the issue of national language education at an earlier stage in primary school. The report also stresses that the Swedish language should become a resource in the construction of the multicultural Finland of tomorrow. Finally, it recommends that the Swedish minority should emphasize innovative technology as one of its representatives, Linus Torvalds, has done. Sticking to a strong and original cultural perspective of one's own, as another Swedish-speaker Tove Jansson, creator of the internationally popular Mumin-characters, is also seen as important (Tankesmedjan Magma [Think Tank Magma] 2010).

For the growing number of immigrants from both EU and non-EU countries, it is obvious that having two national languages presents a challenge (especially when they arrive in Finland later in life). Parents have the right to choose the language of education for their children, and immigrants are free to choose their language of integration as either Swedish or Finnish. But since Swedish-courses for immigrants in Helsinki are difficult to find, even German-speakers are integrated into Finnish instead of Swedish (a Germanic language). Most immigrants also feel the need to study Finnish. On the other hand, immigrants choosing

Swedish find the language easier to learn and tell about warmer attitudes towards them. In a country with an uncertain economy and a growing number of unemployed, fears of climate change and other difficulties, attitudes towards immigrants and minorities have toughened. The growing political support for politicians, who are openly hostile towards foreigners, creates an uneasy atmosphere in which all minorities can become targets for hostility. In order to maintain a sustainable society, it is crucial that poverty, youth unemployment, as well as mental health problems be fought with cooperation on all levels with decisive political leadership. Arguments about the benefit to the country of two national languages need to be addressed, since voices are being raised for Russian instead of Swedish in the schools of Eastern Finland.

More than 300 Finnish cities and municipalities in a country of only 5.3 million people hold a relatively independent position towards the national government since most of the services are produced and provided for by municipalities. The well performing municipally maintained educational system creates equality and possibilities even for children starting out with modest material and social resources.

For the Swedish speakers of Helsinki/Helsingfors, a Swedish educational system on par with the high national standards is required and demands constant development. High quality education presents the best insurance for the future of any society, regardless of the size and status of the group, and regardless of its being the majority or the minority.

References

Association of Finnish Culture and Identity. 2010. *Suomalaisuuden liitto in English* Retrieved from: http://www.suomalaisuudenliitto.fi/?page_id=33 [accessed November 21, 2011].

Björklund, S. and I. Suni. 2000. "The Role of Enlgish as L3 in a Swedish Immersion Programme in Finland," in J. Cenoz and U. Jessner (eds.), *English in Europe: the acquisition of a third language*. Clevedon: Multilingual Matters, pp. 198-221.

Centre for Educational Assesment. 2006. University of Helsinki, *PISA*. Retrieved from: http://www.PISA2006.helsinki.fi/oecd_pisa/oecd_pisa.htm [accessed November 21, 2011].

City of Helsinki. 2010a. *Brief History of Helsinki* Retrieved from: http://www.hel.fi/hki/helsinki/en/Information+on+Helsinki/ Information+on+Helsinki/ [accessed November 21, 2011].

_____. 20101b. *Education.* Retrieved from: http://www.hel.fi/hki/ helsinki/en/Services/Education [accessed November 21, 2011].

Finlex. 2003. *English Translation of Finnish acts and decrees.* Retrieved from: http://www.finlex.fi/en/laki/kaannokset/2003/en20030423.pdf [accessed November 21, 2011].

Hufvudstadsbladet. 2010. "Kiviniemi saknar argument för svenskan" [Kiviniemi lacks arguments for the Swedish language]. *Hufvudstadsbladet*, September 9, p. 1.

Kovero, C. and M. Londen. 2009. *"Språk, identitet och skola" [Language, identity and school].* Helsinki, Finland: Nordica, the Institution of Nordic languages and litterature.

Ministry of Justice, Finland. 2009. *Report of the Government on the application of language legislation 2009.* Retrieved from: http://www. om.fi/en/Oikeapalsta/Haku/1236880953561 [accessed November 21, 2011].

_____. 2010. *Language Act.* Retrieved from: http://www.om.fi/en/ Etusivu/Perussaannoksia/Kielilaki [accessed November 21, 2011].

Tankesmedjan Magma [Think Tank Magma]. 2010. *Det svenska i Finland år 2030 [The Swedish Finland 2030].* Helsinki: Magma.

Tarkastuslautakunta [the Audit Committee]. 2007. *Arviointimuistio ruotsinkielisten helsinkiläisten erityispalveluista [Report on special services for the Swedish speakers of Helsinki].* Heksinki: City of Helsinki.

PART 2: BILINGUALISM IN MULTILINGUAL ENVIRONMENTS

Institutional Bilingualism in Biel/Bienne, Switzerland: Between Identity Politics and Pragmatism

Christina Späti

The town of Biel/Bienne presents itself as the largest bilingual town in Switzerland. Actually, it is the only town which is officially bilingual. Fribourg, the capital town of the bilingual canton of the same name is *de facto* bilingual, but the town representatives have so far refused to acknowledge this fact by granting the town an officially bilingual status. Two other bilingual towns are located in the Canton of Wallis: Sion/Sitten and Sierre/Siders, but, here too, bilingualism has a *de facto*, not a *de jure* status.

Biel/Bienne's bilingualism is an institutional bilingualism according to which public authorities must offer services in both languages, and thus allow its inhabitants to be unilingual. In order to understand the specific characteristics of Biel/Bienne's bilingualism, it is necessary to understand the general linguistic situation in Switzerland, and language policies at the federal and cantonal levels. In a subsequent section of this paper, I will show how bilingualism and the image and understanding of bilingualism have progressed since the 19th century. Relying on several surveys from the last decades, I will demonstrate the popularity of bilingualism in the general public. Finally, I will turn to the question of whether Biel/Bienne can serve as a model for other bilingual cities.

National, legal and demographic context

Switzerland is often considered a model of the successful integration of linguistic diversity (Linder 1998; Schmid 2001). Since its founding in 1848, the country has legally and normatively codified the protection of linguistic diversity and presented multilingualism as a basic component of its national identity. Language policies are legally based on four principles: the recognition of the four national languages, (i.e., German, French, Italian and Romansh); the freedom of language; the principle of linguistic territoriality; and the protection of linguistic minorities (Voyame 1989).

The principle of territoriality is considered to be the most important element of Swiss language policies. As a long-standing, unwritten law, it has been guiding language policies since the early 20th century, giving each geographical region one and only one official language. Moreover, it is generally agreed that the principle of territoriality limits linguistic freedom. It constrains individuals to use only the local official language for purposes of administration, jurisdiction, education, etc. when dealing with the local or cantonal authorities. Thus, the principle of territoriality is often understood as an important measure for the protection of linguistic minorities (Thürer and Burri 2006).

It is interesting to note that Swiss language politics refrain from using the term "linguistic minorities" to depict the smaller language groups. Rather, emphasis is placed on the legal equality of the three major language groups: French, Italian and German (Romansh, the fourth national language, does not have the same legal status as the other three). This has had an important influence on the management of diversity, since it avoids the situation of two or more languages with necessarily a majority and a minority language, and often overtly paternalistic approaches of the majority towards the minority.

In addition to the territorial homogeneity of its language groups, Switzerland has demonstrated a marked stability in its language statistics over the last 150 years. The German-speaking majority of the Swiss population (excluding non-Swiss citizens) regularly amounts to around 70 percent of the population. In the same period of the last 150 years, the francophones have accounted for 20-24 percent, whereas the much smaller group of Italian-speaking people has oscillated at levels between 4 and 6 percent. The Romansh-speakers are the only ones who have consistently lost ground, dropping from 1.7 percent in 1860, to 0.6 percent in 2000, equaling approximately 35,000 citizens (Lüdi and Werlen 2005).

A further characteristic of Switzerland's linguistic landscape is the diglossic situation which can be found in the German-speaking part of Switzerland. Several Swiss German dialects exist alongside a written Swiss standard German which is orally used only for official purposes. Whereas the Swiss Germans tend to value their dialects very highly, their insistence on using them in all possible occasions can sometimes create problems with regard to language politics. This is because the French- and Italian-speaking inhabitants learn the standard variety at school. Therefore, it is not surprising that the propensity to value dialects in German-speaking Switzerland is perceived critically by representatives of these linguistic groups, particularly the French speakers. The increasing use of dialect since the 1970s has often been criticized for undermining national cohesion (Rash 1998).

These general remarks on the Swiss linguistic situation are also relevant to Biel/Bienne. The town is located in the officially bilingual Canton of Berne. Today, the francophones only account for 7.8 percent of the canton's population, the majority belonging to the German-speaking group. The recently completely, revised cantonal constitution includes several provisions designed to ensure the proportional representation of the language groups at all levels, and also contains measures which should guarantee protection of the linguistic minority. Compared to other multilingual cantons, the provisions of the Bernese constitution are considered to be rather accommodating towards the minority (Werlen 2000). Whether these provisions are actually considered to be effective by the Biennoise authorities is, however, a different question.[13]

The town of Biel/Bienne belongs to the officially bilingual district of Biel/Bienne. According to the latest census from 2000, 55.4 percent of the town's inhabitants consider German as their first language and 28.1 percent, French. Six percent are Italian-speaking, followed by various migration languages. With regard to multilingualism, 36.9 percent of the inhabitants indicate that they are unilingual, whereas nearly as much (32.9 percent) are bilingual. Twenty percent are reported to speak three languages or more. Compared to the situation in Switzerland in general, the percentage of bilingual individuals is higher than the average of ca. 25 percent.[14]

Another interesting feature of the town's linguistic characteristics is the high acceptance of the Swiss German dialect among francophones. Whereas in most language contact situations in Switzerland, it is generally agreed that germanophones should switch to standard German when speaking to members of other linguistic groups, the Swiss German dialect is understood and even regularly used by a large percentage of francophone Biennois. According to a recent survey (Longchamp, Bucher, Tschöppe and Ratelband-Pally 2008), 28 percent of the participating francophones indicated that they understand and 23 percent said that they speak Swiss German. Moreover, unlike other institutional bilingual settings such as bilingual cantons or municipalities, the German-speaking members of

[13] In his contribution to this volume, Biennois Municipal Councillor Pierre-Yves Moeschler displays some scepticism with regard to the willingness of the Bernese canton to accommodate the French-speaking minority.

[14] The percentage of ca. 25% of bilingual individuals is valid for Swiss citizens only; the percentage of bilinguals among immigrants is much higher (around 80%) (Franceschini 2003).

the municipal parliament use the dialect in debates, with no simultaneous translation. For this reason, some authors tend to describe Biel/Bienne as tri- rather than bi-lingual (Conrad, Matthey and Matthey 2002).

Biel/Bienne is thus a bilingual town with a German-speaking majority. It is important to note that the German-speaking group is in a majority position at the cantonal level and also at the federal level. Consequently, it is interesting to examine how accommodating this multiple level majority behaves towards the minority group, and whether the two language groups share similar perceptions of bilingualism.

Historical development of Biel/Bienne's bilingualism

At the beginning of the 19th century, Biel was a predominantly German-speaking town. Through the course of the 19th century, it gradually became bilingual, as more and more francophones immigrated from the surrounding region of Jura. They were attracted by the employment opportunities emerging from the town's strong industrialization, particularly in the watchmaking business. By the end of the century, the town authorities acknowledged this demographic change by establishing classes which were taught in French (Kolde 1981).

During the first half of the 20th century, the bilingual character of the town gave rise to several political debates and some anxiety related to linguistic purism. For instance, Gonzague de Reynold, a well known conservative intellectual, declared bilingualism to be a *"signe de decadence"* in 1928 (as cited in Altermatt and Späti 2009: 64). Nevertheless, the Canton of Bern established official bilingualism in Biel/Bienne in 1952, by declaring both German and French as its two official languages (Werlen 2000). However, at that time, the two languages were not fully equal, since the language of the courts was German, as a rule. This inequality, which was rectified only in 1995, shows that the introduction of official bilingualism was a rather laborious process (Richter 2005: 582-583). Since 2005, the town's official name is "Biel/Bienne".

The 1960s were marked by linguistic tensions hitherto unknown in Switzerland. In the French-speaking part of the Canton of Berne, known as Jura, and in close proximity to Biel, a separatist movement emerged which eventually successfully led to the separation of a large part of the French-speaking Jura from the canton and the establishment of the Canton of Jura in 1979 (Hauser 2004). While, to some extent, this movement strengthened the self-confidence of Biel/Bienne's francophones, it did not seem to have had a negative impact on the cohabitation of the two linguistic groups.

The 1970s and 1980s were marked by increased claims by the francophone minority demanding that their equality be better recognized in matters of education and administration. In several interventions in the municipal parliament, they complained about linguistic discrimination and asked for a better application of the town's bilingualism policy. Moreover, at the end of the 1980s and the beginning of the 1990s, the economic downturn in the watchmaking industry was felt much more strongly among the francophone population which, accordingly, suffered more acutely from the rise in unemployment. Many francophone members of the municipal parliament perceived the French-speaking group to be disadvantaged.

The town authorities, thereafter, mandated a report on the language situation in Biel/Bienne which showed that francophones tended to be disadvantaged when it came to jobs in administration (Müller 1987). This resulted in increased criticism of the non-proportional representation of francophones at the senior level of the municipal administration and in demands to establish more apprenticeship places for young francophones. As the statistics published in the annual *Rapport de gestion* of the town show, this indeed has led to an increased and sometimes over-proportional representation of francophones at the senior levels of the administration.[15] At the same time, the authorities increasingly made efforts to commercialize the town's bilingual character. During the 1990s and particularly in the 2000s, the town's representatives successfully presented bilingualism as a major advantage linked to economic progress and individual achievement. For instance, they established the *Forum du bilinguisme* whose main mission is to promote bilingualism (Brohy 2006) and, by doing so, to fulfill the town's economic and financial potential. Moreover, the rising appreciation of individual multilingualism, which could be observed at the national and international levels, also played out in Biel/Bienne. In the last decade, language competencies have become more important as can be seen, for example, in the increased demand for bilingual school programs (Skenderovic and Späti 2009).

To sum up, bilingualism has taken rather different meanings over the course of the years. Whereas it has had a negative influence in the first half of the century and linked to fears of linguistic decline and language loss, it became a notion of contention in the 1960s and 1970s. During this time, bilingualism was predominantly equated with equal language rights of the

---

[15] These statistics were published annually beginning in 1998. See http://www.biel-bienne. ch/ww/fr/pub/administration/administration/conseilmunicipal/chancelleriemuniciapl/ rapports_de_gestion.cfm [accessed November 22, 2011].

two linguistic groups. In the late 1990s and the 2000s, bilingualism came to be seen as a positive aspect with economic and promotional value, which could be used to promote the town's status and attract business.

Public image and everyday practice

Thanks to the rise in public interest in bilingualism since the early 1980s, we can rely on several surveys which were designed to measure its general acceptance by the public. A first survey dates from 1986 (Müller 1987). The question of whether bilingualism had more advantages or disadvantages was answered differently by the two linguistic groups. Whereas overall, the perceived advantages (66 percent) exceeded the disadvantages (13 percent), germanophones tended to value bilingualism more highly than francophones. Whereas the first group perceived bilingualism as rather advantageous by 77 percent, only 58 percent of the second group agreed with this statement, resulting in a significant difference in the response to this question.

The advantages of bilingualism were mainly seen in the acquisition of a second language and the climate of tolerance which bilingualism supposedly fostered. The disadvantages, on the other hand, were seen in problems of communication. More specifically, francophones also listed their unequal status as well as professional disadvantages and a perceived threat to their own culture. Interestingly, 17 percent of the francophones considered their group to be strongly (and 54 percent to be slightly) disadvantaged. This reaction strikingly contrasted with the perception of the germanophone group which predominantly (78 percent) considered the francophone group not to be disadvantaged at all.

A second survey from 1998 (Fuchs and Werlen 1999) showed that the perception of bilingualism had considerably improved in both groups. Now, 80 percent of the germanophones and 72 percent of the francophones estimated bilingualism to have more advantages than disadvantages. Whereas the German-speaking respondents still listed language acquisition as the main advantage of bilingualism, for the francophones, it was now professional advantages which were most positively aligned with bilingualism. This is the effect of the rising demand of language proficiency in the professional domain (Grin 1999). Given the fact that francophones perceive individual bilingualism as an advantage to their professional career, one may assume that the various efforts the municipal council undertook to improve the economic status of the francophone population in the 1990s proved to be rather effective.

The latest survey dates from 2008 (Longchamp et al. 2008) and basically confirms the trends which have already been established. Even though there was a slight decrease in the percentage of respondents who thought bilingualism had more advantages than disadvantages, particularly among German-speaking people, the survey showed that the overall acceptance of bilingualism remained high (72 percent). In particular, the percentage of respondents who saw bilingualism primarily as disadvantageous had decreased. Among the advantages, respondents listed pragmatic aspects such as the simplification of dialogue between citizens, professional advantages, as well as cultural assets such as better knowledge of another culture or the possibility to cultivate tolerance.

Further findings of the survey showed that bilingualism has become more relevant in the workplace in recent years. Fifty-seven percent of the respondents indicated that they regularly use Swiss German at the workplace, whereas 54 percent said they use French. Moreover, 50 percent of the germanophone group regularly speaks French at work, whereas only 37 percent of the questioned francophones use German. It seems as though the French language, as the language of the minority group, is quite well protected. Only 11 percent of the francophones work in a company which is exclusively directed by germanophones. Most importantly, germanophone employees increasingly report working for bilingual management companies, from 24 percent in 1998 to 48 percent in 2008, whereas a similar pattern is observed for the francophones: from 12 percent in 1998 to 35 percent in 2008.

To sum up, the efforts by municipal politicians and administrators to reinforce bilingualism and improve its image among the public have been largely successful. It is particularly important to note that this positive image is not only to be found among germanophones, but also among the smaller group of francophones, even though to a slightly lesser extent. Bilingualism today appears to be widely accepted, not only in terms of a symbolic image of the town to be proud of, but also in everyday life. Some of the former objections to bilingualism can, however, still be observed with regard to immersion and bilingual schools. Given the long history of bilingualism in Biel/Bienne and its general acceptance, it is surprising that, as pointed out in Pierre-Yves Moeschler's paper (in this book), the development of a bilingual educational program is still in its infancy.

Conclusion: Biel/Bienne as a model for bilingual cities?

Biel/Bienne's linguistic situation and its language policies cannot be disconnected from the cantonal and federal contexts. As a part of the national myths, Switzerland's quadrilingualism is generally well accepted among its citizens, and the willingness to accommodate linguistic diversity is traditionally quite high. More important, at the cantonal level, however, is the principle of territoriality with its strong emphasis on linguistic assimilation. This leads to the homogenization of the language groups, and consequently, most Swiss are not confronted with language issues in their everyday life. Institutional bilingualism is well accepted as long as it is confined to a restricted area and has historic roots.

While these aspects of language policy are quite specific to the Swiss linguistic situation, some features of bilingualism planning in Biel/Bienne could profit other bilingual cities. First, the town's authorities have made great efforts in promoting bilingualism as a major economic and cultural asset. This has greatly contributed to the acceptance of bilingualism in recent years, as the various surveys show. However, the causal link between the bilingual image promoted by the administration and the economic success is hard to prove.

Second, the *Forum du bilinguisme* has developed several rather innovative policy measures. Its various activities, as described in Pierre-Yves Moeschler's contribution, play an important role in the promotion of bilingualism. The forum's input is particularly significant in relation to the private sector, which is outside the control of the local authorities. Its main approach is to raise awareness about the importance of equal representation of the two languages in the business sector.

Finally, to a large degree, the relatively high acceptance of bilingualism is the result of constant discussions that have taken place during the last decades in which the two language groups have had clearly assigned roles. The overwhelming majority of parliamentary interventions concerned with language questions during this period came from francophone politicians who felt disadvantaged and sometimes also discriminated against. This led to an ongoing discussion and negotiation between the two language groups. It has also been important that the majority group concedes as much as possible to demands of the minority and assures not only equal, but rather over-representation of the minority at the various administrative and political levels as has partly been achieved in Biel/Bienne since the 1990s. This has been done even more easily since; by chance, the local majority group also represents the majority at the cantonal and federal levels, thus alleviating fears of language shift and language loss. However, bilingualism will most probably remain an important issue on Biel/Bienne's political agenda, and it is certainly possible that the pragmatic compromise that has been found today might be challenged again tomorrow. A further challenge will arise from the question of how to deal with the languages of immigrants, a question that has recently been much debated in Switzerland and which will pose particular problems for bilingual communities.

References

Altermatt, U. and C. Späti. 2009. *Die zweisprachige Universität Freiburg. Geschichte, Konzepte und Umsetzung der Zweisprachigkeit 1889-2006 [The bilingual University of Fribourg. History, Concepts and Implementation of Bilingualism, 1889-2006].* Fribourg: Academic Press.

Brohy, C. 2006. "Perceptions du bilinguisme officiel et interactions bilingues à Biel/Bienne et Fribourg/Freiburg," in D. Elmiger and S. Conrad (eds.), *Le projet bil.bienne – bilinguisme à bienne – kommunikation in biel. TRANEL,* 43: 111-127.

Conrad, S.J., A. Matthey and M. Matthey. 2002. "Bilinguisme institutionnel et contrat-social: le cas de Biel-Bienne (Suisse)," *Marges linguistiques,* 3: 159-178.

Franceschini, R. 2003. "Stimmt das Stereotyp der mehrsprachigen Schweiz?" [Is the stereotype of multilingual Switzerland correct?], in M. Duhem and S. Schmeling (eds.), *Sprache und Identität in frankophonen Kulturen / Langues, identité et francophonie.* Opladen: Leske und Budrich, pp. 101-123.

Fuchs, G., and I. Werlen. 1999. *Zweisprachigkeit in Biel-Bienne. Untersuchung im Rahmen des Bieler-Bilinguismus-Barometers 1998 [Bilingualism in Biel-Bienne. Study within the Bieler-Bilinguismus-Barometer 1998].* Bern: Centre universitaire de recherche sur le plurilinguisme.

Grin, F. 1999. *Compétences et récompenses. La valeur des langues en Suisse.* Fribourg: Universitätsverlag.

Hauser, C. 2004. *L'aventure du Jura. Cultures politiques et identité régionale au XXe siècle.* Lausanne: Antipodes.

Kolde, G. 1981. *Sprachkontakte in gemischtsprachigen Städten. Vergleichende Untersuchungen über Voraussetzungen und Formen sprachlicher Interaktion verschiedensprachiger Jugendlicher in den Schweizer Städten Biel/Bienne und Fribourg/Freiburg i. Ue.* [*Language contacts in linguistically mixed cities. Comparative studies on the preconditions and forms of linguistic interaction among young people speaking different languages in the Swiss cities of Biel/Bienne and Fribourg*]. Wiesbaden: Steiner.

Linder, W. 1998. *Swiss Democracy. Possible Solutions to Conflict in Multicultural Societies* (2nd ed). London, New York: Macmillan, St. Martin's Press.

Longchamp, C., M. Bucher, S. Tschöppe and S. Ratelband-Pally. 2008. *Les efforts en matière de bilinguisme sont payants. Rapport final. Baromètre du bilinguisme de la ville de Biel/Bienne.* Bern: GfS.

Lüdi, G., and I. Werlen. 2005. *Le Paysage linguistique en Suisse. Recensement fédéral de la population 2000.* Neuchâtel: Office fédéral de la statistique.

Müller, C. 1987. *Zweisprachigkeit in Bienne – Biel [Bilingualism in Bienne-Biel].* Zurich: University of Zurich.

Rash, F. 1998. *The German Language in Switzerland. Multilingualism, Diglossia, and Variation.* Bern: Haupt.

Richter, D. 2005. *Sprachenordnung und Minderheitenschutz im schweizerischen Bundesstaat. Relativität des Sprachenrechts und Sicherung des Sprachfriedens [Language law and protection of minorities in federal Switzerland. The relativism of Language Law and the Safeguarding of Linguistic Peace].* Berlin: Springer.

Schmid, C.L. 2001. *The Politics of Language. Conflict, Identity, and Cultural Pluralism in Comparative Perspective.* Oxford, New York: Oxford University Press.

Skenderovic, D. and C. Späti. 2009. "*Sprache und Identitätspolitik. Forschungsbericht im Rahmen des Nationalen Forschungsprogramms 56 Sprachenvielfalt und Sprachkompetenz*" [*Language and identity politics. Research report within the national research programme 56 Language diversity and linguistic competence in Switzerland*]. Unpublished manuscript.

Thürer, D. and T. Burri. 2006. "Zum Sprachenrecht in der Schweiz" [On language law in Switzerland], in C. Pan and B.S. Pfeil (eds.), *Zur Entstehung des modernen Minderheitenschutzes in Europa. Handbuch der europäischen Volksgruppen [On the genesis of modern minority protection in Europe. Handbook on European nationalities]* (vol. 3). Vienna, New York, NY: Springer, pp. 242-266.

Voyame, J. 1989. "Le statu des langues en Suisse," in P. Pupier and J. Woehrling (eds.), *Langues et droit / Language and Law. Proceedings of the First Conference of the International Institute of Comparative Linguistic Law*. Montreal: Wilson & Lafleur, pp. 343-350.

Werlen, I. (ed.). 2000. *Der zweisprachige Kanton Bern [The Bilingual Canton of Bern]*. Bern: Haupt.

Language Planning in Brussels: Two Opposing Policy Mindsets

Philippe Hambye

B russels has long been a magnet for political tension between Belgian linguistic communities. As the capital of Belgium, Flanders and Europe, Brussels is associated with major economic and symbolic issues that make its linguistic and cultural status (a bilingual city, a city whose population is mostly francophone, a multilingual and cosmopolitan city, and a Flemish city) a highly sensitive political issue.

This paper will show how language planning policy in Brussels is determined by a specific organization, namely, the Belgian federal state, and the underlying political vision of that organization, namely, the coexistence of separate, homogeneous linguistic communities. An understanding of that vision is required to understand the actions taken by the various authorities that can have an effect on the city's sociolinguistic situation and ongoing conflicts in and around Brussels.

Institutional context of Brussels

Originally a Flemish city, Brussels started to become French-speaking at the end of the 19th century (Francard 1995) and was mainly francophone by the 20th century. The rise of French was the result of socio-economic and ideological factors: francophones gradually moving to the capital to find work; Dutch-speaking families switching to French, which was the language preferred by employers at the time; and a widespread language ideology that belittled Dutch, reducing it to a "provincial dialect". The city's population is now estimated to be 85 percent to 90 percent francophone. Recent surveys by Janssens (2001 and 2007b) found the demo-linguistic structure of Brussels to be as follows: 50 percent unilingual francophone, 10 percent unilingual Dutch-speaking, 20 percent bilingual (fluent in French plus Dutch or another language) and 20 percent allophone (fluent in neither French nor Dutch).

Strictly speaking, the city of Brussels is but one of 19 *communes*, or municipalities, that make up the Brussels-Capital Region, which is one of the three regions; the other two regions in the Belgian federal state are the Flemish Region and the Walloon Region. The federal entity, which has its own level of authority, Parliament and government, is the only "linguistic region" in Belgium that is bilingual; in the other linguistic regions, only certain *facilités* (or individual rights) are provided to language minorities, and only in locations in which their presence is recognized under a 1963 law.

Official bilingualism in the Brussels-Capital Region differs from official bilingualism in multilingual cities elsewhere, especially Canada. In fact, it is not that Brussels is bilingual, but that the population of Brussels consists of two major national linguistic groups. That is, the philosophy of bilingualism in Brussels is not the philosophy of an entity deemed to be "intrinsically plural" with respect to language and culture, but that of a government body practicing bilingualism for the sole purpose of fulfilling, in a democratic and fair way, its duties to a population that is not linguistically homogeneous.

This situation, which significantly influences language planning (see below), is a result of the political structure of the Brussels-Capital Region. On one hand, "customizable" areas such as education, culture, scientific research and health care are not managed by the Brussels government, but by separate institutions for each linguistic community; each language group manages those areas for its region (Flemish or Walloon) and for Brussels-Capital through organizations that deal with Dutch-speaking and French-speaking persons separately. Therefore, areas with the greatest impact on the sociolinguistic situation in Brussels are, in fact, co-managed by Flemings and francophones. On the other hand, the most important decisions for the future of Brussels (funding of the region, political structure and language laws) are made at the federal level, where opposing Flemish and francophone mindsets clash, without a multicultural, multilingual vision of Brussels ever being expressed.

Therefore, the language planning policy in Brussels is not under the purview of the Municipality of Brussels, which is managed by a large francophone majority (more than 85 percent of the municipal council is francophone). Strict compliance with federal language legislation aside, the municipality could well be managed as a unilingual entity without significantly affecting electoral support for the parties in power.

Language planning policies in Brussels

The main outcome of the institutional context of Brussels, as far as language planning is concerned, is the existence not of *one* language policy, but of *two opposing policy mindsets* and *two opposing policy programs* with respect to the management of language issues in Brussels.

Language policy: francophones

First, let us consider the policies implemented by the francophones through community institutions and, to a lesser extent, municipal institutions, which are mostly under francophone control. For the most part, there is no policy. The francophones do not have an actual language or cultural policy strategy for Brussels. To them, Brussels is simply a region subject to federal official bilingualism legislation that, for example, requires official communications to be in French and Dutch, street names to be selected from both languages, and Dutch to be the first foreign language learned in francophone schools (students in Wallonia have the option of learning English instead). The result of the policy landscape described above is that, aside from administrative services, there is in Brussels not one bilingual network of public institutions and services (cultural centres, universities, schools, nurseries, etc.), but two unilingual networks. Accordingly, a francophone resident of Brussels will receive French-only administrative documents and not bilingual documents. In the private sector, the situation varies: the large number of Dutch speakers working in Brussels, if not living there, has prompted most private organizations (movie theatres, restaurants, businesses, etc.) to provide services in both languages, although French is given greater visibility. Some organizations (media organizations, certain libraries, certain hospitals, etc.) specifically target a francophone or Dutch-speaking clientele. Some neighbourhoods of the capital, which are generally more posh, are more bilingual than others, and the linguistic landscape changes accordingly in the various parts of the city. Furthermore, the presence of European government workers and large numbers of tourists, as well as the desire to avoid the costs of bilingual communications, have prompted the use of English as a third language on some commercial signs.

The demographic weight of francophones in Brussels and their confidence in the future of their community (often perceived as arrogance by Flemings) have allowed them to rest on their laurels and have not motivated them to develop a proactive policy to ensure the survival and development of

French in the capital. It is important here to note that, while francophones are a minority nationally, they do not feel "minorized", as minority groups most often do (Hambye 2009). However, the situation is different in the areas surrounding Brussels, especially in the "municipalities with facilities" in the Flemish Region, which have francophone minorities. The francophone parties have taken numerous positions to defend the language rights of those minorities.

Francophones have also not had to worry about implementing policies on the status of Dutch-speaking minorities, because those minorities are defined and protected by federal policies. These policies were negotiated under a balance of power, that since the late 1980s, has led the francophone parties to agree to institutional reforms sought by the Flemish parties, in exchange for amendments to federal entity funding legislation sought by the south of the country, as a result of economic decline there, which began in the 1970s.

The situation is also the result of the ambivalent relationship between Brussels and Wallonia. Brussels is obviously an important city for Belgian francophones: it is home to the headquarters of political parties, major media groups, numerous cultural institutions, etc. But, it is not the capital of Wallonia (it is instead the capital of Flanders), and it is not necessarily the top priority of all francophones. While Flemings have chosen not to distinguish officially between Flanders and Brussels (an easy decision, since Brussels is located in Flemish territory), francophones must always manage the conflicting interests of two entities in what is now called the *Communauté française Wallonie-Bruxelles*. Since the majority of their electorate is in Wallonia (less than one quarter of Belgian francophones live in Brussels), the francophone parties have not developed a centralist mindset leading to massive investment in Brussels. In fact, there has been a tendency toward decentralization in the last few years. Major cultural institutions are found scattered in surrounding Walloon cities even though Brussels is *de facto* the main cultural hub for Belgian francophones. In early 2010, the leader of the Walloon government even wanted to restart a movement to reinvent the Walloon identity, which makes sense in a mindset of affirmation and opposition to Flanders, but tends to symbolically break the ties between Wallonia and Brussels, and hampers the perception of Brussels as a focal point for all francophones. In addition, wealthy francophone families have long tended to leave the municipalities in the heart of the Brussels-Capital Region (including the municipality of Brussels) and settle in outlying municipalities or even in the Walloon or Flemish regions.

Lastly, it should be noted that, contrary to what is seen especially in Quebec, the linguistic assimilation of new immigrants has never really been a concern for francophones: linguistic and cultural integration policies implemented by francophone institutions have been rare in Brussels (and Wallonia), at least compared to those implemented by Dutch-speaking institutions (see below), because immigrants generally choose French, and francophone parties are reluctant to develop policies that target cultural or linguistic groups; such policies are at odds with the republican political philosophy predominant among Belgian francophones that tends to reject anything resembling multiculturalism or communitarianism (Hambye and Lucchini 2005).

Language policy: Dutch speakers

The policy direction of Flanders with respect to Brussels is vastly different. The Flemish population is, in general, not particularly attached to Brussels: the city is seen as being too francophone, cosmopolitan and multicultural; immigration in Brussels is definitely greater than in Flanders, with people of foreign origin representing 25 percent of the population in Brussels versus only 5 percent of the population in Flanders (Ibid.), and as a place with great insecurity, etc. Therefore, few Flemings (only 100,000 to 150,000 out of 6 million, or approximately 2.5 percent) choose to live in Brussels; however, many work there.

Despite the lack of affection for the capital, Flemish politicians have been working since the 1950s to avoid "losing Brussels" and to ensure that the status of Dutch is maintained and developed in the city. Since 1989 especially, the *Vlaamse Gemeenschapscommissie* (VGC or "Flemish Community Commission") has increased its initiatives to strengthen the presence of Dutch in Brussels (Witte 2009).

To that end, the VGC has invested in providing Brussels residents with high quality nurseries and schools. As in many other places, spaces in nurseries are hard to find in Brussels; therefore, Dutch-language early childhood services are an attractive alternative for francophone parents. The exodus of middle-class families to surrounding areas and the influx of socio-economically fragile immigrants has resulted in the decline of entire neighbourhoods and forms of educational segregation (certain schools being attended almost exclusively by children from poor communities). VGC-run schools are better funded and attract families that are better off socioculturally, and are therefore an attractive alternative for non-Dutch speakers. Those Dutch-language services have quickly become popular with francophone families, which have also become aware of the economic benefits of mastering Dutch in a country with an ever-increasing wealth disparity between the north and the south.

On the strength of its economic growth, Flanders has also invested heavily in Flemish cultural institutions in Brussels and, in a general way, to make the city more attractive for Flemings; for example, bonuses are offered to those choosing to settle in the capital or funding is provided to support bilingualism among health care workers.

More recently, policies aiming specifically to encourage immigrants to learn Dutch have been implemented through the creation of the *Huis of Nederlands* ("House of Dutch"), which is a network of centres providing free Dutch courses, and a regulation introducing quotas on children from poor communities and children of foreign origin in VCG-funded schools. Furthermore, the Flemish government is not stopping there, because already it is believed that the number of spaces in Dutch-language schools will have to increase in the next few years (Janssens 2007a) to handle the population growth expected in Brussels, as a result of positive net migration and a higher birth rate than in other regions.

The sociolinguistic situation in Brussels: issues and challenges for the future

What are the challenges for the future of language planning policies in Brussels? The answer depends mainly on the policy objectives set, such as encouraging francophones and allophones to learn and use Dutch, helping Flemings to settle in Brussels to increase their representation in the city, or preventing the "reflemification" of Brussels, which would be harmful to francophones.

Therefore, the first challenge is to set objectives that are shared by all political players in Brussels, so that their work will be in the interest of all residents (francophone, Dutch-speaking and allophone). The vision of Brussels as a crossroads between Flemings and francophones (Walloons), co-managed by the *Communauté française* and the VGC, has prevented the creation of a network of institutions promoting the development of a multilingual and multicultural city, and has instead led to competition between organizations, reducing individuals to being exclusively francophone or Dutch-speaking.

The key success of the VGC policy has been to promote the emergence of a "community of interest" for bilingualism and restore the popularity of a language long stigmatized by the francophone middle class. In fact, while

Flemish school populations in Brussels decreased throughout the 1970s, 20 percent of children in Brussels today are educated in Flemish nursery schools, in spite of the fact that unilingual Dutch-speakers represent only 10 percent of the population of Brussels (Fonteyn 2009). A survey published in 2007 by Janssens (2007b, 2008) shows that, overall, the residents of Brussels have an attitude toward Dutch that is ever improving.

A number of factors have made that development possible. First is the role played by economic factors. The main component of the Flemish strategy was to repair the image of Dutch through the basic institutions of early childhood services, education and culture: the policy's success is a reminder that individuals are willing to pay for bilingualism if it gives them access to high quality services and resources that would otherwise be unavailable. However, the creation of such incentives requires significant financial investment that only wealthy linguistic communities can make. In addition, the change in attitude of francophones in Brussels toward Dutch is part of a larger but recent trend of francophones learning the Dutch language. Primarily for economic benefits, as indicated by the sudden increase in schools offering Dutch immersion programs in both Brussels and Wallonia, more francophones are enrolling in Dutch language study, some taking advantage of funding from the Walloon government for Dutch language studies as part of the economic recovery policies (Hambye 2009).

Secondly, a key to the success of the VGC is without doubt its choice of an approach promoting bilingualism (rather than defending the interests of Flemings alone). This policy helps dissociate speaking Dutch from belonging to the Flemish ethnolinguistic group. The Dutch language can then be associated more with the bilingual Dutch-speaking community of Brussels, which is viewed as modern, dynamic and open, rather than being associated only with Flanders, which is often viewed as insular (Janssens 2008: 13-14). All residents of Brussels can claim Dutch as a symbol of their specific multilingual and multicultural linguistic identity. Surveys recently commissioned by the VGC on cultural centre users in the Flemish community in Brussels (Van Mensel and Janssens 2006) examine not only Flemish users, but also users overall, which indicates a change in vision in which members of the ethnolinguistic group (Flemings) are considered to a lesser degree than members of the community of interest for Dutch (both Dutch speakers and Dutch language enthusiasts).

That affirmation of a Brussels-specific identity is strengthened by the emergence of a Brussels-specific, citizen-based movement uniting Dutch speakers and francophones on interests specific to the residents of Brussels. This movement, led by prominent figures from the worlds of politics, economics and academia, is attempting to break out of the mindset of Flanders and Wallonia co-managing Brussels. While Brussels is sometimes perceived as a bothersome exception to the mindset of linguistic homogeneity that prevails in the other regions of Belgium, social players in Brussels are trying instead to view Brussels as the crucible from which springs the uniqueness and richness of Belgium as a bilingual country, enabling Belgium to assume its role of (triple) capital, cultural and economic centre. Their aim is therefore to have Brussels managed by its residents, and to meet policy challenges specific to Brussels (regarding mobility, education, population explosion, etc.). Here too, it is the highlighting of concerns shared by francophones and Dutch speakers in Brussels that makes it possible to rise above the division that is growing across the country.

That dissent outside Brussels is the second greatest threat to a successful alliance between the francophone majority and Dutch-speaking minority to manage bilingualism in Brussels. Political conflicts between Flanders and Wallonia, which have seen renewed tension since 2007, are maintaining each linguistic community's fears and feeding the mistrust – or even animosity – between francophones and Dutch speakers within the bilingual region of Brussels. Furthermore, the VCG's approach thus far has been in some ways at odds with the nationalist discourse of many Flemish political parties that have a mindset of confrontation (and not cooperation) with francophones and fear of immigrant communities. Political forces whose *raison d'être* is nationalism are skilfully maintaining a mistrust of the minority and a propensity to defend its own interests exclusively and defensively, to the point that they are preventing policies common to both communities from being implemented in certain areas. For example, in education, the Flemish government is categorically refusing to cooperate with the *Communauté française* to open common bilingual schools for both linguistic groups, thereby limiting the opportunity for francophones (and allophones) to develop a mastery of Dutch, while immersion schools and Dutch-language schools in the city are turning away students because they are full.

Conclusion: lessons to be learned from the situation in Brussels

In talks on language planning, the discussion is sometimes limited to finding the best "technical" solutions to problems with managing multilingualism. Plans are made to use educational methods to improve knowledge of the languages in question (for example, through immersion programs) or implement structures to provide bilingual services to the population more effectively. However, what is the use of learning the other community's language if there is no desire to have any contact with that community? If each group exists with its own networks and institutions, without any real publicly shared space, why bother to learn a second or third language? Why would a minority (since it is usually the minority that learns the majority's language) want services in its own language if it appears that those services merely provide the majority with a way to pay lip service without being truly willing to affirm the fundamentally multilingual character of the political community?

Such measures can succeed only if there is an explicit underlying political vision to which both the minority and the majority can subscribe. The change in attitude of francophones in Brussels toward Dutch is not the result of "best practices," but rather the result the VGC's policy direction and specific social and economic conditions. Although state and civil society do not always have the means to respond to social and economic conditions, they can still try to create a community of interest in favour of their policy plan. As seen in Brussels, it is by changing the values associated with Dutch and the way that the community in Brussels sees itself that players such as the VGC and citizen-based movements in Brussels have managed to revive interest in bilingualism, affirm the legitimate place of Dutch speakers in Brussels, and make the bicultural nature of Brussels an asset rather than a burden.

For the VGC, that was made possible only through political decisions (not very obvious in the Flemish context) to promote the status of Dutch in an open fashion without defending the interests of Flemings. Such a policy changes not only the language planning objectives, but also the way in which the outcome is interpreted. The fact that the number of native-born Dutch speakers in Brussels is dropping would point to failure if an ethnolinguistic approach to the language policy were taken; however, to the extent that Dutch is gaining ground in public, and especially in bilingual families (Janssens 2008: 5), the current trend could be considered as positive from another point of view.

While setting objectives shared by the linguistic majority and minority is a prerequisite to any effective language policy, it is crucial to prevent the distancing of the linguistic groups that sometimes arises in political battles in other areas – a situation the Swiss call *Belgisierung* or "Belgification" (Stotz 2006) – from precluding the development of a common vision. It therefore continues to be necessary to work in advance at bringing the "two solitudes" closer together (Taylor 1992).

References

Fonteyn, G. 2009. "Flemish Education in Brussels: A Success Story," *Bruselo.info*. http://www.bruselo.info/.

Francard, M. 1995. "Nef des Fous ou radeau de la Méduse? Les conflits linguistiques en Belgique," *Linx*, 33: 31-46.

Hambye, P. 2009. "Plurilinguisme et minorisation en Belgique : d'étranges rapports aux langues 'étrangères'," *Langage et Société*, 129: 29-46.

Hambye, P. and S. Lucchini. 2005. "Sociolinguistic Diversity and Shared Resources: A Critical Look at Linguistic Integration Policies in Belgium," *Noves SL* 6. http://www6.gencat.cat/llengcat/noves/.

Janssens, R. 2001. *Taalgebruik in Brussel : Taalverhoudingen, taalverschuivingen en taalidentiteit in een meerstalige stad*. [Language Use in Brussels: Linguistic Distribution, Language Switching and Linguistic Identity in a Multilingual City]. Brussels: VUB Press.

_____. 2007a. *Nederlandstalige verhuizers van en naar Brussel. Een wetenschappelijk onderzoek naar de verhuisbewegingen van de Nederlandstalige bevolkingsgroep in en uit het Brussels Hoofdstedelijk Gewest. Onderzoek in opdracht van de Vlaamse Gemeenschapscommissie.* [The Migration of Dutch-Speakers into and out of Brussels: A Scientific Survey on the Migration of the Dutch-Speaking Population in the Brussels-Capital Region]. Brussels: BRIO. http://www.briobrussel.be/.

_____. 2007b. *Van Brussel gesproken. Taalgebruik, taalverschuivingen en taalidentiteit in het Brussels Hoofdstedelijk Gewest.* [Speaking of Brussels: Language Use, Language Switching and Linguistic Identity in the Brussels-Capital Region]. Brussels: VUB Press.

_____. 2008. "Language Use in Brussels and the Position of Dutch: Some Recent Findings," *Brussels Studies*, 13. http://www.brusselsstudies.be/.

Stotz, D. 2006. "Breaching the Peace: Struggles Around Multilingualism in Switzerland," *Language Policy*, 5: 247-265.

Taylor, C. 1992. *Rapprocher les solitudes : Écrits sur le fédéralisme et le nationalisme au Canada*. Sainte-Foy: Les Presses de l'Université Laval.

Van Mensel, L. and R. Janssens. 2006. *Publieksonderzoek Gemeenschapcentra. Een onderzoek naar het profiel van de bezoekers van de Vlaamse Gemeenschapcentra in Brussel*. [Survey on Community Centre Use: A Survey on the Profile of Users of Flemish Community Centres in Brussels]. Brussels: VUB, Centrum voor de Interdisciplinaire Studie van Brussel.

Witte, E. 2009. "Looking Back on Twenty Years of VGC Policy (1989-2009)," *Bruselo.info*. http://www.bruselo.info/.

Administrative Management and Public Services in Barcelona

Jordi Font and Antoni Rodon

Introduction

The process of globalization has forced all societies of the world to adapt to new challenges and demands. Among these is the necessity to deal with a new sociolinguistic situation, characterized by the need not only to be connected at the international level, but to communicate public information inside the borders of many states which, until a few years ago, were officially unilingual.

Catalonia, and especially Barcelona, through multilingual management, has accumulated assets that have converted it into a multicultural territory as well as into a multilinguistic zone. For this reason, the administrations and the citizenship, in general, have been operating under a complex linguistic reality for decades. Nevertheless, the central questions of this chapter are still clearly relevant: How does the municipality of Barcelona, officially bilingual, deal with the multilingual reality? What is the role played by the official languages, Catalan and Spanish, in the public services offered by the Barcelona City Council? Which services offered by the public sector are multilingual? This text intends to summarize the task carried out by the City Council of Barcelona when managing the multilingual reality of the city.

Our goal here is to describe the linguistic practices in the Municipality of Barcelona and its relationship with the citizenry. Following this introduction, the second section describes the multilingual context of the city, while the third part focuses on its official bilingualism, and the legal and social status of Catalan, which has been designated as a preferred language. The fourth section analyzes the multilingual reality of the municipality from the point of view of the citizen-administration relationship and the fifth concludes this exposé.[16]

Barcelona: a multilingual city

Catalan is a romance language spoken by almost 10 million people in the territories that today form Catalonia, the Autonomous Community of Valencia and the Balearic Islands (besides the state of Andorra and other territories in Aragon, France and the city of Alghero in the island of Sardinia, Italy). It is the eighth language of the European Union, coming before Greek, Portuguese, Czech or Swedish. It is, therefore, not a minority language, neither in European terms nor from an international perspective.

A survey on language uses conducted in 2008 (Statistical Institute of Catalonia 2008) indicates that only 5.4 percent of the Catalan population does not understand the Catalan language. Table 1 shows, moreover, that around 80 percent of the Catalan population speaks and reads Catalan. The same survey indicates that there is also a broad knowledge of Castilian. Almost all citizens are able to understand, speak, read and write it. The metropolitan area of Barcelona has similar figures. The survey also shows that English is the third language in Catalonia. More than 32 percent understand it. French is the fourth language; it is understood by 21.3 percent of the Catalan population and, as well, almost 17 percent speak it and 12.7 percent write it.

TABLE I   Percentage of population with knowledge of Catalan, Castilian, English and French (2008)

	Understand it	Speak it	Read it	Write it
Catalan	94.6	78.3	81.7	61.8
Castilian	99.9	99.7	97.4	95.6
English	32.0	26.4	27.9	24.1
French	21.3	16.7	16.9	12.7

Source: Statistical Institute of Catalonia (2008).

[16] All comments and arguments reported here are from a current project about linguistic practices in the Municipality of Barcelona, titled "Multilingual approach between citizens and the administration". The study carries out an analysis of the printed materials distributed by the municipality, participant observations in different public places and in-depth interviews with civil servants and workers of the city council.

The same survey studied the initial language learned, the language with which the speaker identifies most strongly and the language most commonly used.

TABLE 2   Percentage of population with initial language learned, language speaker identifies with and most commonly used language (2008)

	Initial language learned	Language speaker identifies with	Most commonly used language
Catalan	31.6	37.2	35.6
Catalan and Castilian	3.8	8.8	12.0
Castilian	55.0	46.5	45.9
Arabic	2.6	2.4	1.9
Other languages	6.7	4.9	4.6

Source: Statistical Institute of Catalonia (2008).

Data (see Table 2) show that Castilian is the initial language learned and the most commonly used language for half of the population. "Language speaker identifies with" reveals the same tendency. Catalan is the most commonly used language for 35.6 percent of the Catalan population. Therefore, the percentage of those using Catalan most frequently is below the percentage of people who understand it.

The results also show that 12 percent of the population says they use both Catalan and Castilian. In 2003, the same survey showed that this percentage was 4.7 percent. This suggests that the percentage of bilingual citizens is increasing.

The available data indicates widespread use of Catalan. Nevertheless, Catalan is still the minority language, because it is used less frequently, and mostly in the administration and public services, and in private domains of activity. This situation can be traced back to the Francoist dictatorship (1938-1975) which was hostile to Catalan: it reduced the language to use in private domains and excluded it from official institutions. With the establishment of democracy, as well as important demographic changes, the Catalan administration has restored Catalan "to its place". This was done with strong political and social consensus, accompanied by the creation of important public policies to foster the expansion of its use.[17] This, in turn,

[17] The Catalan government, with a great social and political consensus, initiated the so-called process of "linguistic normalization," which consisted of different public initiatives to boost and protect the Catalan language. For instance, in 1983, the Catalan Parliament approved the first linguistic normalization law.

increased social harmony among the different languages, and protected and consolidated the historical language of Catalonia.

Nowadays, although the integration of the foreign-born population is usually carried out spontaneously in Spanish, Catalan has become a language of reception and a clear sign of integration in the social and political reality of Catalonia. It is seen as a language of social cohesion that favours the equality of opportunity and constitutes a fundamental pillar in the process of cultural integration. This social interest in Catalan is shown by the increase of those who have learned it in the past few decades and the intention of many to learn or improve their use of it (the same survey of linguistic uses reveals that almost three out of four people want to study it).

Like all the important capitals of occidental Europe, Barcelona has also developed as a fully multilingual city in the last few years. The following section describes the population and its main characteristics.

In the last twenty years, the population of Barcelona has had irregular growth. If in 1991 the census registered almost 1,650,000 inhabitants, from 1996 onwards their number diminished. Due to the prices of residences, important segments of the population of Barcelona have abandoned the city and moved to another city or town outside the capital. However, while local residents went outside Barcelona during the second half of the nineties, the city continued to receive new immigrants. The migration phenomenon is crucial to understanding why the number of inhabitants started increasing as of 2001 (Department of Statistics of the Municipality of Barcelona 2010a).

Figure 1 confirms the importance of the growth of the foreign born population. In 2001, the census of Barcelona registered 74,019 foreign persons. In 2003, the figure was twice as high (163,046 persons in the census were foreign). From then onwards, the foreign population has continued to grow. The last figure, for 2009, indicates that almost 295,000 inhabitants of Barcelona are foreign. The foreign born population has gone from 4.9 percent in 2001 to 18.1 percent in 2009.

FIGURE 1 Evolution of the percentage of foreigners in the Barcelona census

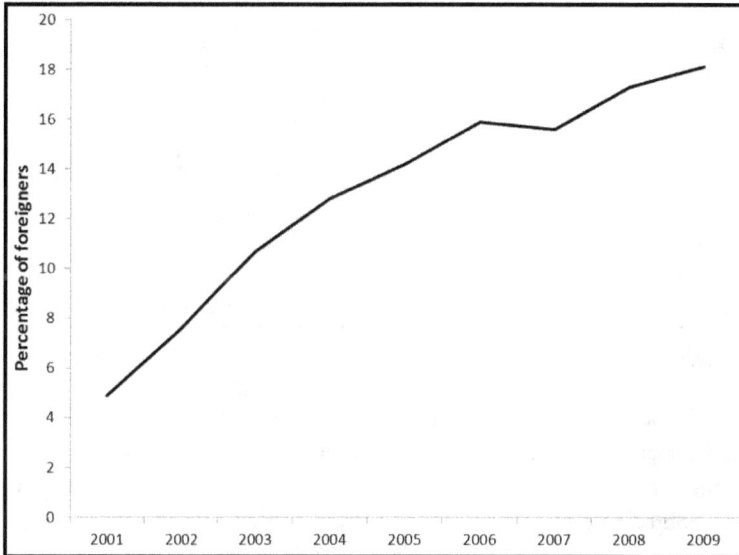

Source: Department of Statistics of the Municipality if Barcelona (2010a).

The arrival of a migrant population has also increased the number of different nationalities (see Table 3). According to the Department of Statistics of the Municipality of Barcelona (2010b), in 2009, 166 different nationalities were represented in Barcelona. The most represented continent is Africa, with 48 different nationalities and a total of 22,283 habitants. Europe is the second continent, both in terms of numbers of nationalities and absolute numbers of people. But in absolute numbers, America (especially Latin America) is the most represented continent in Barcelona, with a total of 127,615 habitants. Among those that are not of Spanish nationality, the main nationalities are Italian (7.9 percent), Ecuadorian (7.3 percent), Pakistani (6.4 percent), Bolivian (5.7 percent), and Peruvian (5.2 percent).

TABLE 3 Number of nationalities and inhabitants in Barcelona (2009)

	Number of nationalities	Population	%
Europe	45	1,430,962	87.4
Spanish nationality		1,337,186	
European nationalities		93,776	
Africa	48	22,283	1.4
America	31	127,615	7.8
Asia	39	56,923	3.5
Australia	3	314	0.0
TOTAL		**1,638,103**	**100.0**

Source: Department of Statistics of the Municipality of Barcelona (2010b).

The arrival of a foreign population represents an additional challenge for Catalan. However, Catalonia has been a country that has historically opened its doors to newcomers who, in turn, have participated in and contributed to its development. In Catalonia almost 72.3 percent of the foreigners understand Catalan (Statistical Institute of Catalonia 2007). Public policies aim to boost the knowledge of Catalan, creating incentives for learning (and using) the concept of "their own" historical language

Catalan: the preferred language

The *Spanish Constitution* of 1978 (Article 3) states that "Spanish is the official language of the State" and the "other Spanish languages shall also be official in the respective self-governing communities in accordance with their Statutes" (Government of Spain 1978).

Taking into account what the Constitution established, the Statute of Autonomy of Catalonia (Government of Catalonia 2006), the basic institutional law of Catalonia, states that "Catalan is the language of normal and preferential use in Public Administration bodies and in the public media of Catalonia, and is also the language of normal use for teaching and learning in the education system" (Preliminary Title, Article 6). "Catalan is the official language of Catalonia, together with Castilian, the official language of the Spanish State" (Preliminary Title, Article 6.2). Following these very high level constitutional documents, the Parliament of Catalonia adopted two laws that regulate the different language policies (*Act 7/1983* and *Act 1/1998*). The former established Catalan as the language of education in primary schools (immersion system), the use of Catalan in public signage and the knowledge of Catalan required to work for public administration and services. The later protected the right of use of Catalan in any domain.

More recently, public administration has taken important steps to consolidate the Catalan language. For instance, the *Education Act* (passed in July 2009) has enshrined the immersion system, which converts Catalan, the language of Catalonia, into the vehicular language in the educational system. The immersion system has received extensive public and political consensus, and has become an important source of social cohesion, since it allows all the students, regardless of the language they speak at home, to finish the compulsory education knowing Catalan and Spanish. This system acts as a "social elevator" and boosts the equality of opportunities among citizens. As a result, the Catalan immersion system has been endorsed by the Council of Europe.

According to the Regulation of Catalan Language (Barcelona City Council 2010), Barcelona is officially a bilingual city, and the Catalan language, as the "own language" of Barcelona and, by extension, of Catalonia, is the pillar of municipal action (Ibid.: Chapter II, Article 2). This regulation also allows any citizen to be served in Spanish, on demand.

The formalization of Catalan as the official language forces the local administration – like all the other administrations – to deal with two challenges. First, from the "demand" point of view, some citizens would request the provision of certain public goods in a different language than the official ones. This has more or less forced the consideration of a multilingual approach while, in parallel, the administration provides the means toward acquiring a basic knowledge of Catalan (mainly) and Spanish.

Second, thanks to the multilingual state of affairs, it is very important to be able to respond quickly to changing linguistic citizenship needs and adapt the supply of services to these needs. In general, the Municipality of Barcelona has developed both proactive and reactive positions. On the one hand, it has chosen to pre-empt the linguistic needs by providing public services with multilingual workers and mediators and also with printed information in several languages. On the other hand, it responds to new situations like deciding which languages will be included in an advertising campaign. Different ways of approaching the multilingual reality, therefore, correspond to different actions, distinguished mainly by internal rules and informal procedures based on experience.

The reality of the multilingual administrative and public services

What is the multilingual approach of the City Council of Barcelona?

Examining the linguistic practices of the municipality shows how the local regulations established in February 2010 are actually operating. For the most part, public communications from the local administration to citizens are carried out in Catalan. It is the most commonly used language for public signage, brochures or flyers or in oral or written communications.

If Catalan is the preferred language in many areas, Spanish is also used, especially when communications with the public require it. The use of third languages depends on the contacts that the service has with migrant populations and the necessity to communicate with groups using languages other than Catalan or Spanish. However, it is possible to identify two models (see Figure 2):

FIGURE 2 Degree of multilingualism as a function of service

Higher multilingual intensity

Education, Health system, Citizen Attention Office, Immigration, CNL, Civic Centers, Local police

Libraries, Innovation, Barcelona TV, Retail, Mobility and Transports

Lower multilingual intensity

Sports, Participation, Environmental Services, Town-planning Services.

+ *Areas with intensive use of third languages*: These services generally take more proactive actions and have acquired some capacity to use third languages due to the constant and intense contact with people with languages other than Catalan and Spanish. It is the case of the intercultural mediation service or the health service, both of which usually deal with many migrants.
+ *Areas with less intensive use of third languages*: These services also use third languages, albeit less frequently. When the situation requires them to be used, the public services proceed to respond in languages other than Catalan and Spanish. Cases in point are city-planning services and environmental services.

Even though some common procedures can be identified across different sectors, it is important to highlight some local practices that are particularly good examples of the multicultural dynamics of Barcelona.

Intercultural mediation service. During 2009, this service performed 25,000 intercultural mediations. Their actions include mediation in the interpersonal sphere – with the goal of guaranteeing mutual communication between public officials and foreign populations, and mediation to solve community conflicts – with the goal of restoring intercultural dialogue and coexistence among cultures. Furthermore, specific training is offered to the public servants regarding the characteristics of the most important non-European migrants (Roma population from Romania, Chinese, Pakistani, North African and South American).

The mediation service has grown in importance and is used in multicultural contexts across different management groups within the city council. The team is composed of four mediators who work in the field, a person in charge of interpersonal mediation, a manager of community mediation and a general coordinator.

Health system. Hospital del Mar in Barcelona is one of thirteen hospitals in the Catalan capital and is located in an area with a high rate of migrant population. About 25 percent of their users are immigrants. The hospital has developed pioneering programs incorporating, for example, the presence of intercultural mediators, which act as bridges between doctors and patients in cases of linguistic problems.

Otherwise, Barcelona has an extensive network of hospitals, health centres and social services. Since the health sector has intensive contacts with different linguistic groups, primary care doctors and the Catalan hospitals have a computer program that allows doctors to communicate with the patients, orally and in writing, in nine languages, including Arabic, Romanian, Urdu and Chinese (the most important languages among the immigrant population in Catalonia). The system, called the Universal Doctor Speaker, translates the common questions of the doctor as well as the patients' answers. The program also translates the treatment and the prescription.

Library service. The main, and almost the only, language in which full public information is available in the Barcelona libraries is Catalan. However, there are abundant materials in Spanish, as well as in other languages such as Arabic, French, Portuguese, English or German, depending on the public that usually goes to a specific branch. Each of them decides which multilingual material to acquire, according to the users' demands.

Citizen Attention Office. Barcelona has eleven citizen attention offices, one per district. These offices exist to answer all the questions and respond to all the issues of the citizens. Catalan is the language used in the initial contact, although the public workers are able to answer in Spanish, French or English. In the central Citizen Attention Office, citizens are served in seven languages, including Arabic, Chinese and Urdu. The application forms and procedures of the office are on the Internet in Catalan, Spanish and English. The office has also printed materials (brochures, leaflets …) in different languages.

Infos idiomes. *Barcelona Televisió* is a good example of the integration of the multilingual reality in the way the local administration works. *Barcelona Televisió* broadcasts *Infos idiomes*, a news program in foreign languages. The information is broadcasted in ten different languages, including Polish, Tamazight, Taixelhit, Finnish or Russian, and is subtitled in Catalan. Thus, the different communities have the opportunity to express their opinion in their own language. The program promotes the values of interculturality and multilingualism. At the same time, it has a clear objective to increase the integration of the migrant population in that it fosters communication networks among migrant communities and allows them to be part of the decision-making process.

These activities and services are described in order to highlight some interesting examples of multilingual management developed by the Barcelona City Council. They show that the city has a strong tradition and important background in the development of multilingual and multicultural approaches. A further example is the celebration in 2008 of the Intercultural Dialogue Year, under which numerous activities took place to promote diversity and the importance of intercultural management. In 2005, the Municipality of Barcelona and the *Generalitat* (executive government of Catalonia) created *Linguamón*, House of Languages, which had a clear goal: to bring language issues closer to the population and to highlight the richness of linguistic diversity as a positive value for our society.

In 2010, all these actions led to the Intercultural Development Plan of Barcelona, a global strategy based on the interaction of different cultures and languages as a way to create diversity in all public spheres.

Conclusions

In addition to the persistent necessity to promote Catalan (extend its use and normalize it in the public sphere), the last decade of the 20th century and the early 21st century have added new linguistic challenges that have made the situation more complex. However, new approaches to multilingualism also entails a stimulating exercise to promote cultural, social, economic and, of course, language diversity.

Like the most important European cities, Barcelona is and will be multilingual. The municipality, with its most important social, cultural and political actors, has established, through broad consensus, that the Catalan language, the "own language" of Catalonia, has a preferential position in any municipal action. At the same time, Spanish is also official, as established by the Spanish legislation. But the preferred public image of Catalan nevertheless does give non-Catalan speakers a reference point and does create incentives for learning and using that language.

The promotion of Catalan in all sectors of society runs parallel to the use of Spanish and other languages, according to the needs in each service area and its level of contact with people who know neither Spanish nor Catalan. The examples highlighted in this paper illustrate this reality.

To sum up, linguistic diversity has become a crucial issue and the City of Barcelona has taken important steps to deal with this new reality. It is an issue that has been raised and will continue to be a challenge for the future to come. In fact, it must be seen as a great opportunity to develop new strategies to accommodate the internal pluralism of the Catalan society.

References

Act 7/1983, April 18th, on linguistic policy. 1983. *Official Bulletin of the Autonomous Government of Catalonia, n. 322, April 22nd 1983. Official State Gazette, n. 112, May 11st 1983.* Retrieved from http://www.twoak.com/bgfd [accessed November 23, 2011].

Act 1/1998, January 7th, on linguistic policy. 1998. *Official Bulletin of the Autonomous Government of Catalonia, n. 2553, January 9th 1998. Official State Gazette n. 36, February 11st 1998.* Retrieved from http://www.twoak.com/bgfd [accessed November 23, 2011].

Barcelona City Council. 2010. "Regulation of Catalan Language," *Official Bulletin of the Province* (February 13). Barcelona.

Department of Statistics of the Municipality of Barcelona. 2010a. *Statistical Yearbook of Barcelona City.* Statistics of population and household. Official figures of population. Evolution of figures. Barcelona: Department of Statistics of the Municipality of Barcelona. Retrieved from www.bcn.cat/estadistica [accessed November 23, 2011].

_____. 2010b. *Statistical Yearbook of Barcelona City.* Population and Demography. Nationality by sex. Barcelona: Department of Statistics of the Municipality of Barcelona. Retrieved from www.bcn.cat/ estadistica [accessed November 23, 2011].

Government of Spain. 1978. *Spanish Constitution.* Retrieved from www. congreso.es/consti/ [accessed November 23, 2011].

Government of Catalonia. 2006. *Statute of Autonomy of Catalonia.* Retrieved from www.gencat.cat/generalitat/eng/estatut/ [accessed November 23, 2011].

Statistical Institute of Catalonia. 2003. *Enquesta d'usos linguistics de la població 2008. Survey on language uses of the population 2003.* Retrieved from www.idescat.cat [IDESCAT (2003)] [accessed January 15, 2012].

_____. 2007. *Enquesta demogràfica 2007 (ED07). Demographic survey 2007 (ED07).* Retrieved from www.idescat.cat [accessed November 23, 2011].

_____. 2008. *Enquesta d'usos linguistics de la població 2008. Survey on language uses of the population 2008.* Retrieved from www.idescat.cat [IDESCAT (2008)] [accessed November 23, 2011].

Biel/Bienne: A Linguistic Bridge at the Language Boundary

Pierre-Yves Moeschler

Biel/Bienne is significant not because of its size (population 50,000), but because it is an example of a major city that is officially bilingual in a country that has raised quadrilingualism to the status of national legend. A major industrial centre, Biel/Bienne is home to famous watch factories found throughout the Jurassian Arc, which lies between Switzerland and France. Names such as Rolex, Omega and Swatch come to mind: these watch brands are located in Biel/Bienne. The precision machinery industry also has a large presence here. In recent times, the economy of Biel/Bienne has diversified into the communications industry. Because the region is mainly export-oriented, businesses in Biel/Bienne and the Jurassian Arc are very exposed to the global economic situation. When the US market sneezes, the entire region catches the flu! As a result, after a number of painful crises, the decision was made to diversify. How does one go from dominating the manufacturing industry to transitioning to the service industry? By building on bilingualism, of course!

The Swiss context

Switzerland is a quadrilingual country. The harmonious coexistence of the four linguistic identities is a source of national pride. However, the Swiss strictly observe the principle of territoriality. The French-speaking Swiss are in the west (Lausanne, Geneva) and the German-speaking Swiss are in the east (Zurich). Bern presents itself as a bridge between the cultures, while Biel/Bienne sits right on the language border. Biel/Bienne is the economic, cultural and educational centre for a metropolitan area with a population of 200,000, exclusively German-speaking in the east and south, and French-speaking in the west and north.

The development of Biel/Bienne is inextricably linked to the history of Swiss watchmaking, which has its roots in the French-speaking Jurassian Arc. Nestled at the foot of the Jura Mountains, the German-speaking city (named Biel in German and Bienne in French) was ideally located to welcome Jurassian business people wishing to settle in the plain, closer to commercial routes and urban centres. The authorities of Biel/Bienne had the foresight to welcome them, as a way of promoting the economy, and established the conditions of their settlement: tax rebates initially, and then education infrastructure and the increasing use of French in political and social life. That took place in the mid-19th century, when immigrants were usually required to integrate, if not assimilate. With the French-speaking people in Biel/Bienne, the opposite was done: they were provided with the means to maintain their identity and therefore reject assimilation. With time, they came to consider that a given, and they still defend their differences and rights vigorously today.

What are the secrets to that success? The transformation of Biel/Bienne from a unilingual German to bilingual German-French city is partly the result of the relationship the Swiss German have with their language. Refusing to be assimilated with the Germans, with whom they have, or rather had, no political connection, they have cultivated their dialects with determination. Standard German is used in written communication. Only reluctantly do they speak it. At a time when French was the international language of choice in Europe, its prestige attracted the Swiss German population, starting with the middle class. Still today some Swiss German speakers would rather speak French than standard German. While dialects make it possible for them to maintain a barrier against Germany, French opens, or rather opened, a door to the world. English has now changed things somewhat, and standard German has made some headway.

The development of the French-speaking community in the 19th and 20th centuries has led to the current ratio of 60 percent German speakers to 40 percent French speakers. Of course, each community has a number of allophones, 25 percent to 30 percent each. An influx of immigrants from southern Europe (Italy, Spain and Portugal), mostly in the second half of the 20th century, and African immigrants today have increased the French-speaking population. However, immigrants from the Balkan countries and Turkey have joined the German-speaking population.

Institutional bilingualism

Gradually, from the beginning of the watchmaking industry in the mid-19th century, institutional practices were implemented that made it possible for the two communities to live together and identify fully with the city. Make no mistake: one can be a German speaker in Biel/Bienne and not understand a word of French, and the inverse is not only possible, but quite common.

The French-speaking population has always had a certain difficulty, if not reluctance, to learn Swiss German, which is not taught in the schools. The basics of standard German that students learn do not enable them to communicate with German-speaking inhabitants of Biel/Bienne, who are reluctant to speak *hochdeutsch*, or "high German." However, regardless of his or her skill level in the other language, no inhabitant of Biel/Bienne feels less of a citizen than the others – such is the level of linguistic tolerance in the city. That is the result of many practices that have developed and become entrenched in laws and regulations that serve, in theory, both linguistic groups. However, they actually serve mainly to protect the French-speaking minority. Therefore, there is, in theory, no official discrimination. A few examples follow.

First, Biel/Bienne has two parallel school systems. French- and German-speaking students attend classes most of which are in the same buildings. However, the students in each class are linguistically homogeneous, immigrant languages aside. Children are educated in the language of their parents. If the family is bilingual or allophone, the parents can choose the language of education. Once that decision has been made, it cannot be changed, because the national French- and German-language curricula are not the same. For foreign language classes, French speakers must take German first and vice versa. A national debate recently took place on the priority that should be given to English. In areas near the language border, the old practice of postponing English studies until students have reached adolescence persists. Basically, the school plays an identity-forming role: it is a mechanism for passing on a linguistic and cultural identity. Bilingual education has only recently been introduced, at the post-compulsory level; both communities, especially the minority group, feel assured that the school remains a bastion of unilingualism, except for recent developments discussed below.

From a legal perspective, both languages are absolutely equal. Legal texts in either language are equally authentic. Each citizen therefore has the right to address the authorities and the public service in either official language and receive a response in that language. While the customer is always right in business, the citizen is always right in public administration in Biel/Bienne: the public service must adapt to the citizen, not vice versa. Public service employees must therefore know both languages, and both linguistic communities must be represented in government bodies, namely, the municipal council (local executive) and city council (Parliament). Out-of-town visitors who sit in on parliamentary sessions are surprised to see that representatives speak in their own language, and there are no interpreters. A representative could make a statement in French and be answered in Swiss German. All members of the government are expected to have passive knowledge of the other language, which has come to be known as the "partner language".

Of course, language skills vary in reality, and each person develops his or her own strategies to understand and be understood.

Institutional bilingualism is less than perfect, naturally. It exists because of unwavering insistence on the part of French speakers that their rights be upheld. Inequalities persist: in particular, there are few French-speaking senior public servants, so that the public service sometimes forgets its obligations, and internal administrative documents are produced mainly in German. Obviously, in areas having direct contact with the public (for example, social services, education, culture and police), both languages are well represented, since the public would not tolerate it otherwise. However, public works and finance are controlled by German speakers, because no one has ensured otherwise, and both areas are shielded from public opinion. Nevertheless, it is the expressed will of the political authorities to strive for proportional representation of both languages in all departments.

What about political representation? The representation of German and French speakers in city council closely reflects their representation in the population. That is the result of chance or, rather, the natural functioning of a proportional democracy. Few parties are unilingual. The Socialist Party (social democratic) has marked the history of this blue-collar city. It has a French-speaking section that joins forces with German-speaking socialists during elections. The same happens with the main conservative party, which is called the Radical Party. The other parties are mixed. There is no regulation to protect the minority, which simply deals with the situation. It generally considers that introducing quotas for the legislative or executive branch would weaken the political clout of its elected representatives. The election of a candidate does not seem truly legitimate if he or she has benefited from special treatment. In recent years, municipal council elections have given rise to passionate debate: the number of full-time members was reduced from five to four to save money. In short, that made the election or re-election of a French speaker to the municipal council rather unpredictable. The population therefore rallied behind French-speaking candidates. Many German speakers were part of that trend, which was ultimately successful. In fact, for many in the majority, a unilingual executive branch is inconceivable. It is possible to go further: for a French-speaking socialist candidate, it is better to rely on the support of German-speaking socialists than the conservative French-speaking electorate – political affinity is stronger than linguistic affinity.

That last statement is significant: it is one of the keys to social cohesion in the bilingual city of Biel/Bienne.

However, the risk of French speakers not being represented on the municipal council recently convinced authorities to revert to a five-seat system, to increase the probability of linguistically satisfactory electoral results. The potential for introducing quotas was again the topic of consultations; despite the mood that prevailed in the city, no one supported that option.

Social and economic bilingualism

Daily life is bilingual. The two linguistic groups are not geographically separate. Almost all school buildings house French- and German-language classes. In everyday life, speakers of both languages coexist. That requires, among other things, that workers in stores be bilingual, at least ideally. The same holds for medical staff, lawyers and public notaries, etc.

Most but not all associations are bilingual. The iconic sports of football and ice hockey are played in both languages, with a small number of minor clubs operating in one language. For some reason, volleyball is played in French and handball in German. One joins a bilingual or unilingual sports club depending on one's linguistic affinity and skill. Therefore, everyone should be able to feel comfortable in Biel/Bienne.

In business and advertising, opinions vary. French speakers often complain that the language skills of salespeople are inadequate or that advertising is mainly in German. That reality can be clearly seen, and the population expects the government to control it. However, legislation and even the Constitution prohibit public authorities from becoming involved in the economy. Any regulation would be contrary to the sacred principle of freedom of trade and industry. It can be seen that globalization and the gradual distancing of economic decision centres have resulted in a loss of awareness of the fragile linguistic balance. How does one explain to a Zurich-based or foreign company that its advertising must be done in two languages in Biel/Bienne? How does one get movie distributors to understand that films should continue to be shown in their original language in Biel/Bienne, with bilingual subtitles in French and German? Local social ownership, which has ensured the satisfactory implementation of bilingualism for so long, is now inadequate. Given the situation, the authorities have promoted the creation of a private law organization, the *Forum du bilinguisme*, whose goals are to observe and promote bilingualism. With its limited resources, it encourages, convinces, exposes and especially discusses with a view to making both languages present in all areas of social and public life. In a way, it protects the two unilingualisms while promoting bilingualism. It also suggests actions to promote the learning of the partner language. One practice that has become popular is the "bilingual tandem," which pairs two people so that they may learn each other's language.

Lastly, the government has the *Conseil des affaires francophones (CAF)*, which is an advisory body consulted by the state each time that the French-speaking population is involved (mainly in the areas of culture and training). In Biel/Bienne, the state is the canton of Bern, which has a population of one million, of which only eight percent are French-speaking. The CAF acted recently to ensure that both languages could be used in the courts, during a trial, and to encourage state action to foster French-language culture.

Consensual bilingualism

"Consensual bilingualism" describes the situation in Biel/Bienne well. The issue of language comes up often in conversations; it is rare for a French speaker not to blow the whistle on some failure in a business or in the government. That can sometimes lead to demands; however, recommendations are usually made that are carefully reviewed and acted upon. Therefore, language issues never lead to open conflict, but rather a common search for solutions to the problems identified. The quickness of French speakers to protest against any breach of their rights is essential to bilingualism. It keeps the Swiss German majority aware of the minority's needs, and it maintains the will, deeply entrenched in the local mentality, to rectify any situation deemed unacceptable.

Language use

The presence of two standards, Swiss German and standard German, have made French speakers reluctant to learn the language of the majority. However, many families are bilingual, and many individuals have learned the partner language in their social or professional lives. Therefore, a significant part of the population uses the other language, at least passively. Although it was stated above that unilingualism was a reality, it should be noted of course that, between the two unilingual extremes of German and French, there are all the possible variants of knowledge of the partner language.

People are often bilingual in Biel/Bienne, but to varying degrees, from vague understanding to passive or active mastery of the partner language. The role of compulsory education is the topic of ongoing public debate. As stated above, it is the bastion of unilingualism. In certain intellectual circles, it has been long believed that learning the other language results in the bastardization of one's own language. That belief was especially strong among French speakers, who were so attached to an ideal of impeccable French that they felt imperceptibly threatened in their cultural identity. That rather common attitude has changed greatly over the last two decades.

For French speakers, the economic crisis in the 1980s brought about the loss of the bastions that were the great watchmaking companies. It became increasingly hard to lead a professional career in French only. For youth especially, finding a job as an apprentice in a company became harder and harder without knowledge of German, let alone Swiss German, as the economy gradually moved under Swiss German control. Given that the Swiss training system relies heavily on companies to train the next generation (under the "dual" system, apprentices are trained in companies and attend "vocational school" only one or two days a week), the situation exposed certain limits of bilingualism. It made French-speaking families aware of the usefulness, if not necessity, of understanding German, particularly Swiss German. Demands were made for children to gain a better mastery of the partner language through school. It was therefore decided that a bilingual education stream would be created in local high schools. Students aged 15 to 18 can receive instruction in both languages. In a given class, half the students are German-speaking and half, French-speaking; half of the courses are taught in German and half in French.

Public opinion is wanting much more. Suddenly, an apparent majority wants the compulsory curriculum to include learning the other language. Bilingualism in Biel/Bienne is viewed as an asset, from which one can benefit only by learning the partner language. For decades, the authorities were expected to guarantee unilingual education; now, they are criticized for not moving fast enough toward the systematic introduction of "immersion" education. A pilot project began in summer 2010 with children who are just starting school. Classes contained a mix of German- and French-speaking students, as well as students of foreign origin. The project was been carefully planned and appeared promising. However, there was resistance from the teaching staff, which had been very cool regarding bilingual education.

Municipal perspectives

In Biel/Bienne, as everywhere, there is the issue of municipal measures influencing the use of languages in the private sphere, the world of economics and trade, and everyday life. Despite limited municipal jurisdiction, "can do" policies must be pursued. The upper political level (namely, the canton of Bern) will not take the initiative. Practically unilingual, it addresses bilingualism only in election speeches, giving itself a testimonial based more on its historical heritage than on the merits of an effective policy. It is up to local municipal authorities to deal with bilingualism. Even though they cannot control the educational system, they can organize schools so that children of both languages meet and share a certain number of intra- or extra-curricular activities. They can make it possible to fight prejudice and pave the way for learning the partner language. Schools are social places; they organize parties, travel, sports events and field trips. All of this activity must involve both linguistic groups, to bring together members of the teaching staff and acquaint students with the other linguistic group, thereby fostering a mindset essential to learning the partner language, which will also be fostered by all of the facilities (nurseries, school cafeterias) and recreational activities available to youth.

Immersion education is also on the agenda. While it is necessary, it must not result in an education stream with special status. The sociocultural composition of bilingual classes must be the same as that of regular classes; otherwise, segregation will increase – a result that education officials wish to avoid at all costs.

The private sector can only be influenced through persuasion and competition: in Biel/Bienne, that is the role of the *Forum du bilinguisme*, which contacts merchants and awards a "bilingualism award". The Forum also grants a "bilingualism seal of approval" to businesses and public service departments that apply and successfully complete a certification process involving strict criteria. Subsidized institutions are bound to the city by service agreements; the payment of public funds is therefore expressly conditional on the practice of bilingualism internally and with the public.

Bilingualism should be promoted as an asset that brings benefit and preserves identity. Those who fear that bilingualism will lead to unilingualism and assimilation must be reassured. Young intellectuals, in particular, must be convinced: the brain drain must be avoided, and people must be invited to move to the city. Biel/Bienne must remain attractive to the linguistic minority: local authorities have a major role to play in that area.

Conclusion

Bilingualism is a part of the historical heritage of Biel/Bienne. It has been a positive experience for German speakers, who consider French as a window on the world. French speakers, more fearful and reluctant with respect to German, have demanded and obtained the protection they were seeking. Balance is maintained, it would appear, but requires constant attention from the authorities and, especially, the people themselves. The increasing economic clout of German is convincing French speakers that knowledge of German is an important asset. Consequently, bilingualism will continue in Biel/Bienne, but care must be taken in handling immigration from around the world.

CONCLUSION

The City as Unequal Refractor

Colin H. Williams

The city of scripture, literature and lore has been variously hailed as the epitome of civilized humanity, idealized as the locus of an undeniable historical destiny and castigated as the site of sin, degradation and exploitation. But if the everyday, banal city is about anything, it is surely about the management of contested spaces and competing interests struggling for recognition, if not always hegemony, in an unequal environment. The most fundamental characteristic of the multilingual city is, of course, the manner in which its constituent languages are managed and refracted by the experience of sharing and suffering from the social organization of city-space. But the city is no mere container; it is not just the theatre within which the main actors of civil society, commerce and governance play their parts. It is, itself, a crucible of change, for within its rhythms and processes, key patterns of language use, promotion, tolerance and conflict are melded. None more so than in the officially bilingual or trilingual city, for the primacy given to one or more official languages is itself a significant determinant of the type and range of activities, and social and public services available in specific languages. Official designation also influences the degree to which other non-official languages will receive some degree of recognition in the governance and management of the city. Thus officially bilingual cities are a distinct sub-set of cities.

In this volume, we have encountered a series of studies which, taken together, offer a rich *mélange* of insights and recommendations regarding the current and future development of selected bilingual and multilingual cities. In this conclusion, I want to provide two services to the reader. The first is to draw out some of the broader implications of the material, data and insights offered above. The second is to identify some challenging and, indeed, exciting policy-related themes for future work in this area.

By definition, the historical context is key to all of the unique situations described in this volume, even if the European cities are of a greater provenance than the Canadian examples. So much of the form and function of the contemporary city has been shaped by past events and processes, which collectively leave a distinct impression on the city's image, character, spatial layout and role in the modern space economy. Some of the cities discussed in this volume such as Helsinki, have a centuries-old provenance, deeply rooted in their regional or national psyche; some, such as Ottawa, represent the heart of their nation, as the primate city or the capital; others, such as Biel, serve as bridges between two or more ethnolinguistic groups and geo-strategic culture zones. Others, such as Barcelona, have achieved global status, have obtained iconic significance and currently face challenges in relation to official bilingualism and immigration adjustment which characterize so many of the cases discussed herein.

I want to argue that in the academic theorising by American-influenced social scientists concerned with city development and growth, language-related issues, while not exactly ignored, have been relatively underplayed, and more often subsumed within broader social categories, such as ethnic groupings, religious affiliations or racial divides. Apart from the realm of education, few city-wide studies have sought to trace the assimilatory contours by which original language loss, as opposed to the language gain mainly, but not exclusively of English, have characterized the late 20th century. There are, of course, exceptionally significant individual case studies of Toronto, Montreal (Levine 1990), Vancouver (Yee 1988) and New York (Garciá and Fishman 2002) among others, which bear close reading for general, as well as discreet inter-generational trends in the language dynamics of city-space, collective organizations and neighbourhood adjustments. However, this current volume is to be welcomed for it offers a systematic comparative treatment of several cities and should serve as a boost to the renewal of interest in urban multilingualism and language policy management.

Discourse regarding the role and symbolic function of language

Competition in the city

In many of the cases discussed in this volume there has been a conscious attempt to overcome the perceived disadvantages of managing city spaces wherein more than one language competes for salience. For much of the 20th century, and earlier where there was a strong municipal system, such 'cultural' issues were conventionally treated as problems, as a sign of weakness, of the mal-integration of the residents who were to be considered more in terms of their productive capacity, their socio-economic needs and their political mobilization. In official discourse today, the language mix of residents is expressed less in terms of a series of problems to be overcome, and more as a rich resource potential to be exploited for the corporate benefit of the city. However, it remains true that in cities, as in states, languages in contact tend also to be languages in competition, if not always conflict.

The prime example of a conflict-generating city is Brussels. Hambye (this volume) has detailed how two opposing policies face each other in the management of Brussels. But it is not a zero-sum game, for the involvement of different levels of government in the specification of services, the allocation of resources and the management of disputes, provides a complex analytical, let alone *realpolitic*, framework. Hambye explains that "customizable" areas such as education, culture, scientific research and health care are not managed by the Brussels government, but by separate institutions for each linguistic community – each language group manages those areas for its region (Flemish or Walloon) and for Brussels-Capital Region through bodies that deal with Dutch-speaking and French-speaking persons separately. In consequence, the areas with the greatest impact on the sociolinguistic situation of Brussels are, in fact, co-managed by Flemings and francophones.

By contrast, the most important decisions for the future of Brussels (funding of the region, political structure and language laws) are made at the federal level, "where opposing Flemish and francophone mindsets clash, without a multicultural, multilingual vision of Brussels ever being expressed." The absence of an overarching, convincing framework and ideology means that the language planning policy in Brussels is not under the purview of the Municipality of Brussels, which is managed by a large francophone majority (more than 85 percent of the municipal council is francophone). In formal constitutional terms, this is in complete contrast to the arrangements in, for example, the region of Ottawa. Brussels functions as a mirror and as a zone of conflict for the whole of Belgium. Its significance in determining state level politics and practices cannot be overemphasised. Thus, in consequence, Hambye is moved to observe that "the main outcome of the institutional context of Brussels, as far as language planning is concerned, is the existence not of *one* language policy, but of *two opposing policy mindsets* and *two opposing policy programs* with respect to the management of language issues in Brussels." A house divided, etc.

What is more remarkable is that Brussels, with all its internal differences and staggering inability to strike a compromise also functions as a relatively effective EU capital, warts and all. And yet it is precisely to these abstract notions that most aspects of conflict resolution are directed. What does this say about the practical relevance of the rational justification for the adoption of best practice principles in language management as with all other areas of EU policy making? The reality of political and social contact is a world away from the theoretical nuances and niceties of academic theories of political philosophy and the rule of law in relation to official languages, majority-minority relations and the competence of EU institutions.

The symbolic and the pragmatic aspects of language policy are often in conflict and the latter tends to be favoured over the former. And yet the symbolic does have a role in the long evolution of achieving linguistic duality as social fact. We saw this earlier in Bourgeois' (this volume) honest assessment of the struggle which the francophone community had with city authorities in Moncton. He argues that "the Moncton declaration focuses on three levels of symbolism, each relating to a different area. Locally, it makes it possible to resolve language disputes in the city. Regionally, it removes a barrier to amalgamation. Nationally, the 2002 declaration raised the social and political profile of Moncton, enabling the city to promote its comparative advantage."

The grudging acceptance of French in Moncton is a good example of stealth politics whereby periodic reformulations of the import of the city's rhetoric regarding official bilingualism do not mask the relative lack of real empowerment which the French-speaking residents were able to enjoy until relatively recently. Struggle, and separate and unequal treatment is still the normal experience of minority official language speakers in far too many ostensible bilingual cities, from Moncton to Cardiff, Abo to Donostia. The political rhetoric must always be calibrated against the action of city authorities mediated by the experiential reality of citizens. But it need not be thus, and the more positive message emanating from this volume is that a genuine commitment to official bilingualism can bear fruit to the mutual satisfaction of most of the citizens who can choose which of the official languages they might employ in their dealings with civic authorities and with each other.

In this volume, we have seen evidence where several cities have celebrated their official languages as a positive element adding to the quality of life of residents. Indeed representatives of Biel/Bienne argue that far from being a permanent issue of conflict, representing a negative and irritating factor, as it is in Brussels, a well constructed bilingual policy can actually enhance the vitality of the constituent unilingual communities. In Biel/Bienne, "the new policy protects the two unilingualisms by promoting bilingualism". This is a very positive feature of democratic representation, not unlike the approach of consociational accommodation as practiced in historically religiously-divided societies such as the Netherlands. Providing a clear and consistent overarching bilingual framework, within which all officially recognized language communities can be nurtured, is a major boost to civic harmony.

In a related fashion, Commissioner Graham Fraser has averred that municipal bilingualism, as it is practised in Ottawa, should be perceived as an asset that deserves to be promoted, rather than merely a question of regulation or a device to reduce tension. For him, and many others charged with the articulation of linguistic duality as social fact, bilingualism is a symbol of openness and inclusion that cities can use to distinguish themselves from their neighbours. This is the language of the unique selling point and cumulative competitive advantage, a theme to which we will return below. But promoting linguistic duality is also a means for the officially bilingual city to engage and empower its residents to take pride in their city's achievements and to help shape its policies by 'buying in' to the concept of a responsive and vibrant city. This is certainly the message which comes from Commissioner Fraser, for

> ... by placing linguistic duality at the heart of its identity and image, a city encourages language communities to participate fully in its social, cultural and economic life, and inspires citizens and visitors alike to discover its many treasures. Approaching municipal bilingualism as an asset to be promoted requires strong leadership and the ongoing cooperation of municipal authorities, the private sector and the community. Everyone must participate because everyone stands to gain. Promoting linguistic duality such that it becomes an integral part of a city's image and identity leads to major commercial, economic and cultural returns. It also fosters tourism and makes inhabitants feel proud to live in a city that reflects who they are. The benefits go beyond the merely symbolic (Fraser, this volume: ii).

Best practices

Turning from the city as a locus of conflict to the city as an exemplar, as a model of high quality, not to say self-proclaimed, excellent bilingual services, we may ask questions regarding the arrangement, management and form of the services provided. For example, do the principles of official linguistic duality and of co-equality of treatment of languages necessarily imply a separate but equal dispensing of services to each of the official language networks? Or can co-equality in principle be translated as 'separate fit for purpose' services, rather than a mere duality of city functions and responsibilities? In a similar vein, do bilingual cities typically co-ordinate their bilingual services from a central department which has cross-cutting responsibility, or do each of the language communities interact with their own separate, but parallel, institutional organizations within the city infrastructure?

Burry (this volume) has demonstrated how Ottawa strives to offer a best-practice solution to the satisfaction of the needs of both official language communities. There are many positive lessons and insights contained in this interpretation which would repay imitation in several other settings in Canada, let alone beyond these shores. But one overarching lesson provided by Ottawa is that equality of treatment does not necessarily require a slavish imitation of services and obligations in both languages. Burry argues that

> ... when the city seeks to offer services of comparable quality, it not only recognizes the equality of both language groups, but also the fact that these groups have different social structures and dynamics. Municipal services need to be designed in such a way as to meet the varying needs of different communities. In other words, a service in one language is not necessarily a carbon copy of a service offered in the other language (Burry, this volume: 38).

The two examples offered are both robust; the first is in relation to the cooperation with the two local French language school boards which have been more active in setting up child care programs for pre-schoolers and after-four activities for students than their English language counterparts.

A second example offered was the public health and public transit initiatives which developed culturally sensitive campaigns and programs of comparable quality, rather than imitative translation strategies alone. Yet Burry acknowledges that bilingualism is not given enough weight right from the start of planning processes. Neither do elected representatives and city managers necessarily embrace the bilingualism policy at all times, and yet, it must surely be argued that senior management leadership, the improved training and recruitment requirements of staff and a more balanced investment in an infrastructure which supports operational bilingualism are necessary precursors if the City of Ottawa is to honour its obligations not only to the francophone community *writ* large, but also to its increasingly internally differentiated population, characterized as it is by a greater racial and ethnic source area of birth and origin prior to migration to Ottawa. How these obligations are realized will be a real gesture of faith in the future of an increasingly multilingual and multicultural resident population.

Deep within the construct of an officially bilingual city we may question to what extent the city managers and politicians are actually committed to the concept and practice of multilingualism as a defining characteristic. To put it in its most stark form, we should query to what extent multilingualism is really on the radar of officially bilingual cities? Thus, in terms of bilingual cities as a sub-set of metropolitan areas, we could investigate whether the experience of running an officially designated city actually makes a profound difference as to how officially bilingual cities deal with the demands of the other languages utilized within the city, as compared with other types of cities. Are the non-English, non-French oriented residents of Ottawa served in any manner different than those who live in London, Ontario or Halifax, Nova Scotia? Is Ottawa's experience of city and regional planning likely to make the city authorities more sensitive to the contours of multilingualism?

Bi- and multilingual education

We have seen that official designation, national and city-level legislation and political vision are all influential on the input side of the official bilingual city equation. Thus providing opportunities to use one or more languages through these various structures and agencies is a *sine qua non* for the daily functioning of a bilingual city. But how are various sections of the community empowered and encouraged to take advantage of the opportunities provided? The central anchor of bilingual socialization is the statutory education system and, in her interpretation of contemporary Helsinki, Maria Björnberg-Enckell (this volume) is at pains to stress the absolute necessity of a highly regarded bilingual education system, both for the reproduction of Swedish in Helsinki and for the economic improvement and upward social mobility of pupils. Unlike Canada or Catalonia, where education is a provincial and regional-level responsibility, in Finland it is at the municipal level that the 300 Finnish cities and municipalities discharge their educational and teaching responsibilities. This means that, in theory, children can receive a quite variable educational experience depending on which municipality or rural district they inhabit. For the Swedish speakers of Helsinki/Helsingfors, "a Swedish educational system, on par with the high national standards, is required and demands constant development. High quality education presents the best insurance for the future of any society regardless of the size and status of the group, and regardless of being the majority or the minority." This is quite a remarkable statement, as it gives primacy and a great deal of responsibility to the teaching profession, not only to deliver high standards, but also to guarantee the place of Swedish within the national capital and beyond. And yet it is not so remarkable, for we have seen in nearly every context, ranging from Moncton to Barcelona, that the field of education is one of the most vital and contentious battlegrounds for the expression of group interests. Recall that in the case of Biel/Bienne, Späti (this volume) observed that objections to bilingualism were focussed on opposition to immersion and bilingual schools which are still in their infancy. Yet, in most cities covered in this volume, bi- or multilingual education remains a key mechanism by which the children of immigrants and migrants themselves (through adult education programs) are socialized into one or more of the official languages of the city and of the world of work and social life.

Administrative autonomy

A second critical feature of the Finnish system is the relative independence and autonomy exercized at the municipal level. Of course, there are national level acts which specify the minimum standards of language service delivery, the most recent being the reformed *Language Act* of 2004. The purpose of the act is to ensure the constitutional right of every person to use his or her own language, either Finnish or Swedish, before courts and within other authorities. But the Finnish system specifically provides that an authority may offer better linguistic services than that which is required in the act. Each authority supervises application of the act within its own area of operation. An authority shall ensure, in its activity and on its own initiative, that the linguistic rights of private individuals are secured in practice. The Ministry of Justice supervises enforcement and application of the act and issues recommendations in questions related to legislation on national languages; as well, each electoral period the government reports to Parliament on the application of language legislation and on the securing of linguistic rights. The government also appoints a delegation for language affairs that supports the implementation of the act. Thus the Finnish model provides very clear guidance on a citizen's constitutional rights and how municipal authorities are to discharge their responsibilities. Finland may not have the active offer principle which is engrained within the Canadian

114

system, but it does have a robust system of official language area designation by local authorities and the system appears to work well.

Späti reminds us of the congruence of the multi-layered federal and cantonal politics which bear heavily on the internal dynamics of Biel/Bienne's linguistic situation and states that its language policies cannot be disconnected from the cantonal and federal context. A major factor in conflict reduction has been that institutional bilingualism is well accepted in Switzerland as long as it is confined to a restricted area and has historic roots. A second feature has been the active pursuit of wise and innovative policy measures, as described in Moeschler's (this volume) contribution, where a significant role is allocated to the *Forum de bilinguisme*'s bridge-building and partnership activities with the private sector, where the importance of equal representation of the two languages in the business sector is constantly stressed. If partnership between local authorities, the private sector and the voluntary sector is one source of strength, another is the accommodating attitude and consequent behaviour of the majority populace towards one or more indigenous Swiss minorities. This accommodative behaviour is based on the consensual and largely harmonious political settlement which characterizes the Swiss Confederation. But there is no guarantee that such accommodation will be extended to the management of the issue of the languages of immigrants, a question that has recently been much debated in Switzerland and which will pose particular problems to bilingual cities and communities. Over and above this, there is the more pressing issue of how the European Union and its associated members will deal with the free-flow of migrants and labour within its Schengen Agreement. The latest challenge to mobility pressures comes as a result of the haemorrhaging of displaced populations from Tunisia, Libya and Egypt, and the consequent increase in illegal migration into southern Europe, resulting in the Italian and French governments clashing over the temporary suspension of the Schengen Agreement, and proposing the closer proctoring of border traffic and migratory movements and the whole question of enforced return migration.

Immigration

As a case in point, it is quite a different challenge to devise strategies appropriate to the maintenance of an officially sanctioned language, such as Catalan in Barcelona, while simultaneously targeting the recent immigrants to socialize and integrate into the mainstream of the local, dominant language group (Boix, Cots and Rufo, this volume). Today the city authorities struggle with the twin impulses of social democracy: the efficiency argument which demands that most immigrants acquire some knowledge of Catalan so as to gain employment and a tolerable chance of being accepted within the Catalan civil society, and the equality argument, which argues that most immigrants should be free to choose to affiliate themselves with the Castillian linguistic realm if that is their preferred option. But with what long-term consequences for the vitality of Catalan as the "llengua pròpia"?

Font and Rodon (this volume) provide a realistic portrait which is supported by their daily experience of being heavily involved in Catalan language acquisition by immigrants. The three critical questions are posed at the outset, namely: How does the municipality of Barcelona, officially bilingual, deal with the multilingual reality? What is the role played by the official languages, Catalan and Spanish, in the public services offered by the city council? Which services offered by the public services are multilingual? These are answered in a positive, if guarded manner. They argue that despite the very strong and purposeful attempt by the Catalan administration to restore Catalan "to its place," the struggle for acceptance is not yet over. Since 1975, there has been strong political and social consensus, accompanied by the implementation of innovative and bighting public policies to guarantee social and economic opportunities for the restoration of Catalan. In large part, these successive programs and campaigns have led to social harmony among the different languages, and protected and consolidated the historical language of Catalonia. The twin pillars of this movement have been firm political commitment and empowering legislation.

The abiding message is that the bilingual city is not a closed system, sufficient unto itself. The task now is to articulate those methods by which a greater understanding of the better features of operating a constructive and additive bilingualism can be transferred to other cities desirous of establishing official bilingual status. But first it would be advantageous to identify some of the more promising lines of research which would improve the understanding and possible implementation of realistic city policies in this field.

Research agendas and their application

The mapping of language dynamics

An earlier attempt at mapping out a research agenda for the multilingual city was made by Williams and van der Merwe (1996) in which the potential for geo-linguistic application and multivariate analysis was demonstrated by reference to a geographical information system (GIS) analysis of Cape Town, South Africa. Suggestions for future advances made in that paper have now been realized as social fact, particularly the suggestion that the geocoding of languages within a universal standard classification system be adopted and that linguistic landscaping, using desktop GIS technology, be developed in a large number of cities. We argued this for two reasons: first because it was a significant research tool in its own right for interpreting dynamic changes; and secondly because it promised to open up the city space for the edification of the citizens themselves.

The most innovative application of this concept is that undertaken by Monica Barni and her team in Sienna. Barni (2008) argues that the host-immigrant interaction in major Italian cities is in acute need of fundamental description before even considering policy applications. Her investigations seek to map the new collective linguistic space so as to achieve four aims. The first is the identification of those factors which encourage or work against language maintenance in contested city spaces. The second is to measure the degree of tension which exists between unification/homogenization and diversification in very specific locales within a chosen city. The third is to identify the levels of interaction between host and immigrant along a range of linguistic dimensions, identifying as it were the rules of engagement, adaptive behavioural coping strategies and communicative choices. The fourth is the greater specification of the distinction between migrant languages and immigrant languages, that is, the functional and emotional role which both types of language situation represent in relation to the long-term linguistic cohesion of the community and its prospects for integration into the larger multilingual reality.

Were such studies used to record and identify fine-grained differentiation within the dynamic spaces of other cities worldwide, then a much clearer pattern of the characteristics and needs of the resident populations would be obtained. This geo-database has obvious benign applications for educational policy, health care delivery systems, commercial property and housing conditions, and targeted campaigns by the city authorities. The advance of GIS and computer-aided mapping has allowed for a more comprehensive and powerful means to visualize, simulate and display information in its true spatial context. Its potential in geo-linguistics and linguistic landscaping is enormous, even if its use is rather limited at present (Williams 2009).

Metropolitan multilingualism

A second promising line of research well worthy of emulation elsewhere is the Multilingual Cities Project (MCP) (Extra and Yağmur 2008). The aim of the MCP is to identify the character of metropolitan multilingualism in 20 European cities. The project used a sophisticated language survey questionnaire to assess issues of language vitality and inter-generational transmission of the twenty significant languages under scrutiny. Apart from rehearsing the very special role of French in Brussels and other conventional results regarding the presence of indigenous European languages in major cities, the study did reveal a quite distinct profile for two pairs of languages which are often in competition in their source countries, i.e., Turkish and Kurdish in Turkey, and Arabic and Berber in Northern African countries (in particular, Morocco). Only in Gőteborg was Kurdish more strongly represented than Turkish, and only in The Hague was Berber and Arabic represented in balance. In their database, Kurdish hardly emerged in Brussels and Madrid. The same was true as regards Berber in Gőteborg and Hamburg (Ibid.: 147). The significance of such large-scale multi-city research investigations is not lost on EU and national policy makers and specialist concerned with educational achievement, literacy and numeracy within specific contexts, let alone social cohesion and the reduction of group violence and social dislocation.

Assessing ethnolinguistic vitality

A third promising line of research is a revised form of ethnolinguistic vitality theory (EVT) (Ehala and Yağmur 2011). A consistent message emanating from those who have used the Giles, Bourhis and Taylor (1977) EVT framework, is that the core elements of status, demography, institutional support and control factors underestimate the actual vitality of selected minority groups (Yağmur 2011). Ehala (2011) argues that the subjective ethnolinguistic vitality questionnaire (SEVQ) results ranging from Istanbul to Helsinki do not depend on the immediate sociolinguistic environment, nor the ethnic media usage and the extent of bilingualism, but do correlate with the perceptions of inter-ethnic discordance. This seems to cast doubt on what exactly the SEVQ is, in fact, measuring. Ehala distinguishes between 'hot' and 'cold' prototypical modes of operation whereby members of a 'hot' group are characterized more by their emotional and collective involvement in the shaping of their own institutions, than would be allowed by the 'objective' findings of SEVQ alone (Ibid.: 189). If this is true, this insight has purchase for the manner in which distinct language groups within the official multilingual city react in different ways to the same core common impulses and communicative strategies adopted by city authorities. A significant contribution to the field of public administration and bilingual service delivery systems would be to test this insight with regard to members of both official and non-official language groups.

City governance

A fourth research area relates to city governance and the measurement of bilingual service delivery in cities such as Helsinki, Dublin and Cardiff. Sandberg, Ó Flatharta and Williams (2011) undertook independent research to identify the principal characteristics of language policy regimes in Finland, Ireland and Wales, including the three capital cities. The research was designed to measure to what extent language legislation had been put into practice in terms of the range and quality of public services which citizens obtained. The picture painted is very mixed and the quality of the service provided is inadequate considering that it is reinforced by statutory obligation to be exercised by metropolitan and local authorities. The examination of language laws and related language schemes carried out since 2005 suggests that there are four main reasons for non-compliance (Ibid.). The first is the lack of an institution's capacity and resources to deliver services. The second is the lack of buy-in from senior management. The third is the internal communication of commitments, often lacking or not sufficiently explicit with few guidelines and deadlines set. The fourth is the poor monitoring and review processes regarding the implementation and updating of the language schemes. Recommendations on how to improve this situation were contained in Sandberg et al. (2011) and for Wales are detailed in Williams (2010). Of course, Canada has a long tradition of evaluating public services and the recent work of Cardinal (2008) and her associates: Cardinal and Cox (2007), Cardinal, L., S. Lang, N. Plante, A. Sauvé et C. Terrien, (2005) and Cardinal and Juillet (2005) in relation to francophone identity, and health and legal services, is an obvious and fruitful point of departure for further comparative studies.

But what is lacking both in the chapters collected within this volume and several of the other studies identified above is a consistent, time-series evaluation of the range and quality of the bilingual services on offer in terms of customer experience, and staff expectations and training requirements. Episodic overview snap shots of the structure and function of bilingual health or leisure services, while useful in the absence of anything else, do not come near to the systematic evaluation of city-wide bilingual services across all policy and service-related departments. This comprehensive, holistic monitoring is expensive, but essential, so as to provide regular evidence of performance-related initiatives and constant feedback to the policy makers and implementers, let alone arming citizens with key data indicators and trend analysis.

A second area of weakness in the above studies is the over-reliance on the duties, obligations, rights and expectation aspects of delivering bi- or multilingual services in officially bilingual cities, and the under-playing of the costs involved. This criticism should not be interpreted as an attack on such services, quite the opposite. We seem well able to cost and to argue for the increased expenditure required to maintain the city's 'built' infrastructure, such as its main thoroughfares, parks and gardens and the like. But there is woeful disregard of factoring in the real cost of providing linguistically-differentiated services as a citizen norm. Streets, lighting, sewage, parks and public amenities are mainstreamed expenditures, whereas language is not treated as a public good in official discourse. It has not yet been fully integrated in far too many of the cases described above, despite Graham Fraser's correct judgment that linguistic duality can offer a competitive advantage and a source of collective satisfaction and, even arena, for innovation in service-delivery. The positive elements of sound language planning, identified by Fraser, should not be ignored nor taken for granted, for they are a constant reminder that high levels of satisfaction in the quality of public services derive from hard work and enlightened leadership. "Managers will set a good example by using the preferred language of the people they are addressing. This kind of behaviour fosters a sense of belonging and reinforces linguistic identity, while promoting harmony among citizens – essential ingredients to everyone's happiness."

IT in the bilingual city

A fifth promising area for future research is the interplay between IT and the creative industries, as regards the bilingual cities represented above. Precisely because we have been concerned with both physical and social communication in the impact of the bilingual city on its environs and the rest of the state's economy, we need to be alert to the potential for greater wealth-creation and opportunities which investment in the digital economy of the multilingual city affords. Many such cities act as hosts to significant media hubs and national telecommunication systems.

Because effective creative industries' policies operate in partnership with public and private industries, the bilingual city has a huge role to play in the advance of the delivery of the digital economy and culture. This can range from making 'brown site' land available, to attracting inward investment through preferential rate and corporate tax negotiations, to highly effective inter-departmental coordination by city authorities to anticipate strategic growth and transform potential into reality. The key is good governance and trust, but the commodities are ideas and culturally challenging practices.

The linguistic landscape

This final point is also an important fulcrum for more intense research and investigative activity within this field of comparative metropolitan multilingualism. Of interest would be an analysis of how developments within the thematic area of linguistic landscaping interacts with architectural trends in form and function and whether or not the semiotic landscape of bilingual public buildings actually resonates with members of the public who are not members of either of the official language communities. Are they blind to one or more of the official languages? How do they negotiate access to spaces which appear to 'belong' to one or other of the official language communities? Detailed work on the image of the city as seen through various eyes: local, national and international, would surely pay dividends, as would a more thorough understanding of the experiential city, a city of opening and closing, of formal and informal sectors, of diurnal and seasonal activities. Clearly there is an incipient danger in defining language as a key to social inclusion and of exaggerating the actual role of official languages in the everyday life of citizens. But within officially designated bilingual cities, the separate provision of linguistically-oriented services allows both language groups to access a different range of leisure activities and swimming clubs for children and young adults in Ottawa, and of healthcare facilities, residential care homes and social clubs for the older residents of Biel. I would argue that providing distinct institutional, leisure and welfare facilities encourages the maintenance of opportunites which support the regular use of the non-hegemonic official language and thus strengthens the attempt to realize equality as a social fact.

Conclusion

Challenging days lie ahead for all the cities represented in this volume, the more so as members of the less-powerful official language communities and other non-official target languages ask awkward and hard-hitting questions which reflect the so-what, cynical and critical charges levied against governments and language policy agencies. Underlying this presumption is a conviction that many official agencies do not have the full support of the power of the state and their respective city-regions in protecting, promoting and regulating targeted minority languages. And herein lies the central philosophical conundrum between equity arguments – derived from social justice and democratic theory perspectives, and efficiency arguments derived from long-standing instrumental and managerialist perspectives – the most dominant of which recently has been the dictates of the neo-liberal assumptions behind public service reform, internal market competition and the rolling back of the state in transferring responsibility for certain functions back to the community and its third-sector organizations.

Cities are drivers of change; the more enterprising multilingual cities can experiment with language, education, labour and mobility policies which may be at variance with the state-wide practices or in advance of them in terms of providing a working model that can be emulated elsewhere within the new space economy. But in order to interpret these changes adequately, new transdisciplinary perspectives are needed which go well beyond the 19th century derived concepts of identity, 'majoritarian' and 'minority' languages, all of which have to do with rationalists conceptions which ultimately derive from the power and the legitimacy of the state. The case study illustrations in this volume have demonstrated that more liquid, fluid concepts of the self in social context are needed if contemporary multilingualism is to be managed, let alone harnessed for the benefit of the majority of residents.

Maintaining official bilingual cities is a challenge of social engineering. It demands sound governance and the construction of a shared ideal. But even in Canada, which has a long and proud history of creative accommodation, critics such as Paquet (2008) have pointed to the structural strains which inevitably accompany the maintenance of cultural diversity. Coping rather than controlling, managing rather than steering, seem to be the order of the day. "For the time being, no public philosophy appears capable of providing the necessary inspiration for the reconstruction of new solidarities" (Ibid.: 128). This admission is not a recipe for despair, but a necessary precursor for a more honest, perhaps modest set of narratives, by which our linguistic identities are governed. The grand debates of late 19th century and mid 20th century political theory and social reform have given way to more pragmatic and refracted visions of the future.

Newer theories and arguments suited for the 21st century stress the implementation of transculturalism, inspired by a vague philosophy of cosmopolitanism. A cosmopolite is one who is free from the constraints of city, provincial or state-wide prejudices, a citizen of the world. But the world is too much with us, and for the poorer, disadvantaged and linguistically illiterate and excluded citizens of major cities, how their lives are refracted by the policies pursued in order to maintain the hegemony of official languages is a most certain test of the sufficiency of democratic deliberations and good city governance.

References

Barni, M. 2008. "Mapping Immigrant Languages in Italy," in M. Barni and G. Extra, (eds.). *Mapping Linguistic Diversity in Multicultural Contexts.* Berlin: Mouton de Gruyter, pp. 217-244.

Cardinal, L. 2008. "Les minorités francophones hors Québec et la vie politique au Canada: comment combler le déficit démocratique?" in J.Y. Thériault and A. Gilbert (eds.). *L'espace francophone en milieu minoritaire au Canada : nouveaux enjeux, nouvelles mobilisations.* Montréal: Fidès, pp. 385-429.

Cardinal, L. and R. Cox. 2007. "La représentation des femmes au sein des groupes minoritaires : le cas des femmes francophones vivant en milieu minoritaire au Canada," *Les Cahiers de la Femme,* 25: 91-96.

Cardinal, L. and L. Juillet. 2005. "Les minorités francophones hors Québec et la gouvernance des langues officielles au Canada," in J.-P. Wallot, (ed.). *La gouvernance linguistique : le Canada en perspective.* Ottawa: Presses de l'Université d'Ottawa, pp. 157-176.

Cardinal, L., S. Lang, N. Plante, A. Sauvé and C. Terrien. 2005. *Les services en français dans le domaine de la justice en Ontario : un état des lieux.* Toronto : Ministère du procureur général de l'Ontario.

Ehala, M. 2011. "Hot and cold ethnicities: Modes of ethnolinguistic vitality," *Journal of Multilingual and Multicultural Development,* 32: 187-200.

Ehala, M. and K. Yağmur, (eds.). 2011. "Ethnolinguistic Vitality," *Journal of Multilingual and Multicultural Development*, 32, whole issue.

Extra, G. and K. Yağmur. 2008. "Mapping Immigrant Languages in Multicultural Cities," in M. Barni and G. Extra, (eds.). *Mapping Linguistic Diversity in Multicultural Contexts*. Berlin: Mouton de Gruyter, pp. 139-162.

Garciá, O. and J.A. Fishman, (eds.). 2002. *The Multilingual Apple: Languages in New York City*. Berlin: Mouton de Gruyter.

Giles, H., R.Y. Bourhis and D.M. Taylor. 1977. "Towards a Theory of Language in Ethnic Group Relations," in H. Giles, (ed.). *Language Ethnicity and Intergroup Relations*. London: Academic Press, pp. 307-348.

Levine, M.V. 1990. *The Reconquest of Montreal*. Philadelphia: Temple University Press.

Paquet, G. 2008. *Deep Cultural Diversity: A Governance Challenge*. Ottawa: University of Ottawa Press.

Sandberg, S., P. Ó Flatharta and C.H. Williams. 2011. *From Act to Action*. Helsinki: Svenska Kulturfonden.

Williams, C.H. 2009. "European Union Enlargement and Citizen Empowerment," in S. Pertot, T.M.S. Priestly and C.H. Williams, (eds.). *Rights, Promotion and Integration Issues for Minority Languages in Europe*. Basingstoke: Palgrave, pp. 1-22.

_____. 2010. "From Act to Action in Wales," in D. Morris, (ed.). *Welsh in the Twenty-first Century*. Cardiff: University of Wales Press, pp. 36-60.

Williams, C.H. and I.J. van der Merwe. 1996. "Mapping the Multilingual City: A Research Agenda for Urban Geolinguistics," *Journal of Multilingual and Multicultural Development*, 17: 49-67.

Yağmur, K. 2011. "Does Ethnolinguistic Vitality Theory Account for the actual value of an ethnic group? A Critical Evaluation," *Journal of Multilingual and Multicultural Development*, 32: 111-120.

Yee, P. 1988. *Saltwater City*. Vancouver: Douglas and McIntyre.

Titles published by INVENIRE BOOKS

12. Richard Clément et Caroline Andrew (sld)   2012
     Villes et langues : gouvernance et politiques
     Symposium international

11. Richard Clément and Caroline Andrew (eds)   2012
     Cities and Languages: Governance and Policy
     International Symposium

10. Michael Behiels and François Rocher (eds)   2011
     The State in Transition: Challenges for Canadian Federalism

9.   Pierre Camu   2011
     La Flotte Blanche : Histoire de la Compagnie de Navigation
     du Richelieu et d'Ontario, 1845-1913

8.   Rupak Chattopadhyay and Gilles Paquet (eds)   2011
     The Unimagined Canadian Capital:
     Challenges for the Federal Capital Region

7.   Gilles Paquet   2011
     Tableau d'avancement II : Essais exploratoires sur la
     gouvernance d'un certain Canada français

6.   James Bowen (ed)   2011
     The Entrepreneurial Effect: Waterloo

5.   François Lapointe   2011
     Cities as Crucibles: Reflections on Canada's Urban Future

4.   James Bowen (ed)   2009
     The Entrepreneurial Effect

3.   Gilles Paquet   2009
     Scheming virtuously: the road to collaborative governance

2.   Ruth Hubbard   2009
     Profession: Public Servant

1.   Robin Higham   2009
     Who do we think we are: Canada's reasonable
     (and less reasonable) accommodation debates

To order these books, please contact Commoners' Publishing at
sales@commonerspublishing.com

www.ingramcontent.com/pod-product-compliance
Lightning Source LLC
Chambersburg PA
CBHW052136270326
41930CB00012B/2911